NOT JUST A REALLY GOOD HUMAN

DWIGHT J. OLNEY

NOT JUST A REALLY GOOD HUMAN
Copyright © 2021 by Dwight J. Olney

All rights reserved. Neither this publication nor any part of this publication may be reproduced or transmitted in any form or by any means, electronic or mechanical, including photocopying, recording or any information storage and retrieval system, without permission in writing from the author.

Unless otherwise indicated, all Scripture quotations are taken from the Holy Bible, New Living Translation, copyright © 1996, 2004, 2015 by Tyndale House Foundation. Used by permission of Tyndale House Publishers, Carol Stream, Illinois 60188. All rights reserved. Scripture quotations are from the ESV® Bible (The Holy Bible, English Standard Version®), copyright © 2001 by Crossway, a publishing ministry of Good News Publishers. Used by permission. All rights reserved. Scripture quotations taken from the (NASB®) New American Standard Bible®, Copyright © 1960, 1971, 1977, 1995, 2020 by The Lockman Foundation. Used by permission. All rights reserved. www.lockman.org

Print ISBN: 978-1-4866-2195-8
eBook ISBN: 978-1-4866-2196-5

Word Alive Press
119 De Baets Street, Winnipeg, MB R2J 3R9
www.wordalivepress.ca

Cataloguing in Publication may be obtained through Library and Archives Canada

This book is warmly dedicated to my three beautiful grandchildren: Theo James, Libby Lynx, and Rusty Wren. As you grow up in this world, with many forces working against your Christian faith, may you always know the joy and comfort of the good and sovereign God who made you, loves you, and always works for your best. May you also learn early in life that *your best* in this complicated life is rarely found on easy roads.

CONTENTS

Acknowledgements	vii
Introduction	ix
Setting the Stage	xi
What's the Problem?	1
Is There an Easy Answer?	7
What's in It for Me?	17
Whose Fight Is this Anyway?	27
Questions for God - Round One	35
Questions for God - Round Two	49
Questions for God - Round Three	63
With Friends Like These…	79
A Tale of Two Paths	93
Theological Insights of a Young Eavesdropper	109
A Whirlwind of an Encounter	123
How the Story Ends/Begins	137
Reflections	145
Final Thoughts	153
About the Author	159

ACKNOWLEDGEMENTS

It is with heartfelt gratitude that I recognize the kind and generous people who assisted me in this project.

First, I would like to thank Word Alive Press for selecting my manuscript as the winner of the 2021 Braun Book Award for non-fiction. I appreciate your support for aspiring authors and your dedication to publishing good literature that proclaims God's truth in a dark world.

I also want to thank the gracious congregation of Coteau Hills Bible Church in Mortlach, Saskatchewan. Your enthusiasm and support of my messages encouraged me to turn a simple sermon series into a published work with a powerful, unified theme.

Thanks to my wonderful daughter, Kristen, and my good friend, Chuck Brandt, who read earlier versions of the work in order to reassure me that I was on track and that the theme was working. Thanks also to Kristen and my other lovely daughter, Heather, who helped me clean up my final submission for the Braun Book Awards.

I am also very grateful for the amazing literary talent of my editor, Evan Braun, who is able to make my writing tighter and cleaner than what naturally comes out of my brain.

And finally, thank you to my wife, Jeanette, for not only staying by my side for over four decades, but for always being my biggest fan in the writing process and for teaching me how to love and trust God with faith like a child.

INTRODUCTION

There may be no greater challenge to one's faith in God than having to endure a shattered life. Anguish weakens every human faculty. The way forward is dark. God's reputation comes into question. And we are tempted to think the unthinkable—must pain and evil be welcomed as part of the sovereign plan of a good God?

Welcome to the Book of Job.

This ancient tale of a righteous man's suffering displays the most typical human response to seemingly undeserved hardship. Questions percolate. Maybe God is not that good after all? Maybe he's weaker than we've been told?

When we suffer, God's stock swiftly declines. When the hurt hits home and we assess the measure of our own personal pain, we often treat God like he is a human who has let us down.

Unknowingly, we possess a faulty tendency to imagine God as a top-of-the-line model of humanity, an extremely good version of ourselves. Not with regard to his creative role of course; we readily accept God's pre-eminence in that department, as did Job and his friends.

But consider how God's reputation comes under attack when we assess his moral rule of the universe. We are quick to use divine terms to describe God as the sustainer of the stars, but then we use human terms to evaluate him in our own circumstances, particularly when they're lousy.

In today's western culture, safety is key. God's critics only see him as good if he's committed to his creatures' perpetual safety. When bad things happen to nice people, we are stunned, bewildered, and then angry. It's hard for us to embrace the mystery of the paradox.

It was hard for Job. He just wanted the pain to go away, or at worst for God to make an appearance and explain the situation. But God had a different agenda.

Surrendering to God's sovereign agenda is never easy. It requires a tall order of humble submission. And as Job learned, the path to get there is often long and arduous.

But as we'll see, the heat of Job's fiery trial will forge a great man into an even better man. By the end of his trial, Job will no longer see God merely as a predictable cosmic dispenser of rewards and punishment, but as he truly is—the infinite, mysterious, omniscient, omnipotent, and compassionate sustainer of the universe.

The intriguing nature of the Book of Job beckons us to participate in the saga and learn some unadulterated humility alongside our hero. It is a well-established fact that for our lives to be truly impacted, we need a story. We are drawn to personal narratives because stories have the power to change us as we join the protagonist in the struggle.

As we take this journey together, with all its intriguing subplots, we will also have the choice to embrace a deeper understanding of God's transcendent greatness.

By the end of the saga, the message will be clear: God is incomparably different from us. Not only do we need to revere his unmatched supremacy compared to human wisdom, reason, and conduct, but we also need to humbly surrender to his benevolent sovereignty.

SETTING THE STAGE

In the C.S. Lewis novel, *The Lion, the Witch, and the Wardrobe,* four children—Peter, Susan, Edmund, and Lucy—pass through the wardrobe's portal to find the kingdom of Narnia imprisoned under the spell of the White Witch. Aslan the lion, the king of Narnia, is nowhere to be found. Although rumour has it that he is on the move, he appears to have abandoned his kingdom to the White Witch, who spends her leisure time turning the inhabitants into lawn statues.

The four children set out to explore this strange new country that is locked under evil's spell. They come upon Mr. and Mrs. Beaver, a husband and wife still faithful to Aslan. The Beavers assure the children that Aslan is about to return to set things right. They also speak of a prophecy that suggests the children will have a very important role to play in Aslan's kingdom.

Pondering this baffling yet exciting news, Lucy and Susan's thoughts are drawn to Aslan's character. What is he actually like?

"Is—is he a man?" asked Lucy.

"Aslan a man!" said Mr. Beaver sternly. "Certainly not. I tell you he is the King of the wood and the son of the great Emperor-Beyond-the-Sea. Don't you know who is the King of Beasts? Aslan is a lion—the lion, the great Lion."

"Ooh!" said Susan, "I'd thought he was a man. Is he—quite safe? I shall feel rather nervous about meeting a lion."

"That you will, dearie, and no mistake," said Mrs. Beaver; "if there's anyone who can appear before Aslan without their knees knocking, they're either braver than most or else just silly."

"Then he isn't safe?" said Lucy.

"Safe?" said Mr. Beaver; "Don't you hear what Mrs. Beaver tells you? Who said anything about safe? Course he isn't safe. But he's good. He's the King, I tell you."[1]

---

[1] C.S. Lewis, *The Lion, the Witch and the Wardrobe* (London, UK: Fontana Lions, 1980), 75.

WHAT'S THE PROBLEM?

One cannot help but be both absorbed and bothered by the Book of Job. The early chapters of the drama draw us in. Job's initial faith response is captivating, as are the perplexing implications of a sovereign God who would choose to take such a good man down such a difficult path.

For sincere travellers who desire to make their way through the story, challenges emerge. Ploughing through the dialogue between Job and his friends is laborious. At times, the language is dark and depressing, and the friends become boring by repeating themselves.

Even when God makes his presence known and speaks directly with Job, he is far less sympathetic to the suffering saint than he would be if a human had written the script singlehandedly. And although the last chapter of the book provides the happy ending we all crave, a lot of questions remain unanswered. We may not feel fully satisfied.

Now, to be fair to God, this dissatisfaction probably has more to do with faulty human thinking than with God himself. Suffice to say that the biggest theological problem for humans will always be the inclination to mould God into a human image rather than the other way around.

Regardless, from a human standpoint, it's not unrealistic or evil to say that the Book of Job provides at least as many questions as answers.

Perhaps that's why few travellers venture into this territory for any prolonged period. The Book of Job is a challenging piece of ancient eastern literature written thousands of years ago, containing both prose and poetry. Much of the imagery is of another era and not easily grasped by the modern western mind.

Even though it doesn't outline easily like one of the Apostle Paul's New Testament letters, and even though Christians don't readily turn to its pages for personal devotional time, those who wander into its domain are captivated by this book and its themes. Who at one time or another hasn't asked God, "Why did this happen to me?" For centuries, people have cried out to God, pleading for an answer to this question while agonizing in pain, weeping in grief, or languishing over loss.

Humanity suffers an excess of adversity and heartache—emergency major surgery, a protracted terminal illness, the premature death of a child, divorce, suicide, a wayward teen, a loved one critically injured in a car accident, a child born with brain damage, a major setback in business, a sudden loss of possessions by fire, earthquake, or flood… and because we are rational beings, we hunger for explanations.

If we could see a direct relationship between suffering and sin in our lives—definite connections between our tragedies and our transgressions—the balance of the equation would put our minds at ease. Or so we think. But all too often, problems intrude without explanation. And when we cannot link misfortune directly to known acts of misbehaviour, we conclude that our afflictions are undeserved.

"What did I do to deserve this?" This common wail of despair reveals a sense of injustice, a feeling that the problems we experience at times exceed what is rightfully owed us.

I'm not sure where the notion comes from, but we are inclined to think that life *should* go well for us, generally. Perhaps we were told by someone we trusted, or maybe it's just a natural human tendency, but we're reluctant to give up on the idea that we deserve a certain level of comfort in this life.

Regardless of the source of this presumptuous paradigm, it could be argued that the Book of Job provides the most intense example of undeserved suffering in all literature.

Right out of the gate, we hear that Job is a fabulous guy. And yet, essentially in no time at all, this wealthy and godly man loses everything he holds dear. Adding insult to injury, his friends accuse rather than console, while God remains conspicuously quiet. And even when God speaks to Job out of the whirlwind, Job doesn't get the explanation he repeatedly claims he deserves.

While many people make commendable statements about Job and the book that recounts his story, relatively few know him very well. Typically, people cite with admiration Job's idealized endurance and most quoted lines: *"I know that my Redeemer lives"* (Job 19:25) or *"Can the dead live again?"* (Job 14:14).

Yet this image of Job as a model of persistent endurance is distorted. He must not be seen merely as an Energizer Bunny who keeps on going and going, nor simply a visionary of eternal life that ultimately remedies the unjust suffering of human existence.

No. For much of the book, Job is a mess. And his messiness is what makes the book so valuable.

The story maintains its meaning for the average suffering soul because it presents a total package of a person's struggle. His questions and impatience are afforded even more time than his affirmations. For to know Job's endurance without his protest, and his affirmations without his agonizing struggle for meaning, is to not know Job at all. Job's questioning of the value of faith and his search for the reality of God amidst a nightmare are the points at which we can most readily identify with him.

The Book of Job is not a simple book. It's not one that, in the end, applauds pious platitudes. We don't walk away with any useful religious clichés. Even though we are given more insight into the drama than Job received, we are still left with many questions when the story is done. Was this test necessary? Are such tests a regular occurrence in the courtroom of heaven? Is all human suffering initiated by divine providence or does some bad stuff just happen because we live in a fallen world? Are natural disasters part of God's plan or do weather systems just do their own thing? Why is there such disparity in the level of suffering different people are called to endure? Why does some anguish just never end? Can there be any redeeming value in a tragedy like the Holocaust? Can we really view God as good when he allows awful things to happen to good people? What do we do when God seems silent in response to our cries for help? And, as noted above, what do we really deserve in this life?

Again, the Book of Job evokes as many intellectual problems as theological answers. But that's okay, because it demonstrates that God can handle human questions, even emotionally charged ones.

In fact, confused and angry cries to God are a critical part of processing human suffering. Remember, God is the one who made us rational beings, so it's not a crime to try to make sense of things when life begins to unravel. And it is part of the human package to feel strong emotions when things don't seem logical or fair.

Such scenarios beg the big question: how do we keep our faith in God when our lives go down the toilet?

To say that Job is puzzled by his circumstances is an understatement. At times, he's almost out of his mind in pain and confusion.

Much of human suffering is bewildering and baffling. And because this book deals with the universal mystery of seemingly unmerited misery, ultimately it is a book about faith. Faith in God.

But as will become evident, Job will need to enlarge his spiritual vision. He will be called upon to muster up a new level of belief and trust in a very big God who isn't confined to the realm of proper human behaviour. What will be demanded is not faith in a God who is just a really good human, but rather faith in a God who is the great and glorious Creator, Sustainer, and Judge of the universe.

Ultimately, the Book of Job will only make sense to those who are prepared to enlarge their view of God. Hopefully, the musings to follow will help accomplish that.

IS THERE AN EASY ANSWER?

The age-old question never seems to go away: how can evil and suffering be present in a world that is supposedly governed by a good God?

Most people refer to this question as a *problem*. And since theologians love to solve problems, they have repeatedly explored various avenues to make sense of the issue.

This exploration is no trivial matter, for many people lose their faith over the question. For some, the *problem* is just a confirmation of their predetermination that a loving and powerful God does not exist.

For countless others, though, it is a real struggle. As hard as they may try, they cannot justify rationally the coexistence of an all-powerful good God alongside the travesty of terrible things happening to nice people. If God does exist, they determine that he is either not good or he's not strong enough to intervene in our affairs.

Because this puzzling and ostensibly contradictory image of God is so different from what they believe they were taught somewhere along the line, many just throw out the whole package and settle into some version of atheism—or agnosticism, at best.

To combat this drift away from the Almighty, well-meaning thinkers work hard to present God in a more agreeable manner. Recently, I read a fresh attempt by a contemporary theologian to more pleasantly harmonize the coexistence of a good God alongside torturous human suffering. Because it relates to the subject at hand, and because you might read the book yourself some day, I think it is wise to discuss it at some length.

The proponent of this new paradigm is Thomas Jay Oord, and his book is entitled *God Can't*. Yes, you read it correctly—*God Can't*. The subtitle of Oord's book is "How to Believe in God and Love After Tragedy, Abuse and Other Evils." In the book, he details the tragic stories of many people he has counselled over the years. He chronicles their attempts to solve the problem of evil as it relates to their personal situations and their relationship with God.

The introduction of Oord's book goes something like this. A person experiences an extremely terrible event, such as rape, abuse, miscarriage, debilitating depression, or the death of a loved one. Someone in their circle of faith tries to encourage them by telling them that God loves them and has plans for them that can't always be understood. The victims are told that God allows pain and suffering for some greater good. The abused or hurting soul then must wrestle with how their horror is part of some good plan. Or they may end up wondering if they are even on God's radar at all. After painful deliberation, many conclude, *If God allows evil that he could have stopped, what good is he to us? Even parents will try to protect their kids from harm that is preventable.*

Criticizing the traditional Christian belief that God allows pain and suffering for some greater good, Oord writes,

> In this view, the malevolence of the past is required for the beneficence of the future. Or at least God thinks it's better to allow horrors and holocausts than to prevent them. If God has allowed all past abuse, pain and suffering for some greater good, nothing has ever occurred that God considers genuinely evil. God must have permitted every rape, torture, betrayal, murder, deception, corruption, incest,

and genocide as part of some good plan. From this twisted perspective, evil is good.²

He goes on to say,

I... can't believe all abuse, pain and tragedy are necessary. Not everything happens or is allowed for some divinely appointed reason. It doesn't make sense to say a loving God permits evil. We don't need to say, "Your rape happened for a reason," and mean, "God allowed it." We don't need to believe God allows children to be tortured or think God permits cancer. And so on. We can believe painful experiences and horrific tragedies make the world worse than it might have been. And God didn't want them.³

Oord is convinced that some pain is pointless. In his view, many tragedies have nothing to do with God's plans. They are simply caused by genuine evil in the world. He is particularly critical of the standard Christian clichés used to console the suffering: "God needed another angel in heaven's choir; God wants to make you stronger; God's ways are not our ways; or, everything happens for a reason."⁴

Barring the heaven's choir line, many Christians are convinced that there's a measure of truth in such stereotypical responses. No one these days is comfortable with fatalism. If you believe in God, you obviously want to believe that things happen for God's purposes.

But that's a tough sell to a victim of repeated sexual assault who now wrestles with relational dysfunction, depression, guilt, fear, and hatred of men. Her reflection on the matter might follow this line of

---

² Thomas Jay Oord, *God Can't: How to Believe in God and Love After Tragedy, Abuse and Other Evils* (Grasmere, ID: SacraSage Press, 2019), 12–13.
³ Ibid., 13.
⁴ Ibid., 9.

thought: *My eleven years of abuse was God's plan for my life? I don't get it. How does the horror of rape make me a better person? Couldn't God think of a nicer way to improve my character? And if he could have stopped the abuse, why didn't he? How could he just watch it all those years and do nothing about it?*

Oord's answer to these types of questions is simple. He says, "God can't." God can't prevent abuse, tragedy, and evil singlehandedly. He is not able to stop wickedness by acting alone. So it is pointless to blame God for your suffering because he could not have prevented it anyway. It just happened because of sin and the presence of evil in the world.

Elaborating on his thesis, Oord provides two reasons that allegedly account for God's inability to control the vile events within creation.

On the silly side, and hardly worth a rebuttal, Oord says that it's because God is spirit, and he doesn't have appendages to physically restrain anyone from doing anything.[5]

On the more intelligent side, Oord argues that the strength of his claim lies in the biblical declaration of the fact that God is love. Referencing the realm of human relationships, Oord explains that love and control are complete opposites. Spouses in a marriage should not try to control one another. And because love does not control, a *loving* God does not *control* his creation. In his words,

> When I say God "can't" prevent evil, I mean God is unable to control people, other creatures or circumstances that cause evil. Because God always loves, and God's love is uncontrolling, God cannot control... God's love governs what God can do... I am not placing limits on God. Rather, God's loving nature determines, shapes, or governs what God can do... Constraints to God's power don't come from the outside.[6]

---

[5] Ibid., 31.
[6] Ibid., 26–27.

In defence of this line of thinking, Oord quotes the Apostle Paul's words in 2 Timothy 2:13: *"[God] cannot deny himself"* (ESV). So, because God's primary nature is to be loving, he cannot control. To perform acts of both love and control in his interaction with humans would constitute a contradiction within his very essence. The limits of God's power come from God's loving nature. Obviously, says Oord, a loving person—especially a parent—makes every effort to prevent preventable evil. So, since God is love and he doesn't prevent a lot of evil, it must be because he cannot do so.

I must confess, when I first started reading his theological paradigm, parts of it began to resonate with my heart. Something about it felt right.

But when I stopped feeling enamoured with the wistfulness of my emotions and re-engaged my brain, some serious concerns readily emerged. Yes, I understand the relational problems that arise when one spouse in a marriage has control issues. But to say that love and control are complete opposites is oversimplistic. To say that a loving person cannot have control over a situation is just plain silly. Life is more complex than that.

Contradicting his own theory, Oord himself suggests that kind and loving parents frequently try to control the behaviour of their young children to keep them safe, to prevent them from getting hurt unnecessarily. Even in a loving marriage, a devoted spouse will try to use their influence to nudge their partner in a healthy direction if they are currently on a harmful path.

Now, before I get too far into my critique of this sincere man's theory, he does deserve some kudos for his efforts.

It is prudent to mention that Oord lays out what he believes to be five main points involved in understanding and processing human suffering. That God cannot prevent all evil singlehandedly is just his first point. His other four points are:

1. God feels our pain when we suffer.
2. God is always at work to heal our pain.
3. God faithfully squeezes good from the bad things that happen to us.
4. God needs our cooperation to do the good work of healing he wants done in people's lives.

I believe Oord speaks a lot of truth within the context of his last four points. For example, I appreciate what he has to say about the role believers need to play as God's hands and feet in the good work of his eternal Kingdom. As the African proverb says, "When you pray, move your feet." Christian prayer should not just implore God to fix problems of pain and suffering when, tangibly, believers themselves could be part of the solution.

I also like what Oord says about the ongoing presence of God in his creation. Those who call upon the Lord to intervene in a hurting person's life often forget that he is already there, always. God is omnipresent, continuously working for our good in every situation. He does not *enter* a situation from the outside as if he were previously away on other business.

As well, regarding the logistics of bringing relief to the suffering of hurting souls and abuse victims, I agree with Oord's tenet that God works alongside all healthcare workers. Whether they be counsellors, chiropractors, massage therapists, nurses, surgeons, or your hairdresser, the good work of God is always a part of human healing, even if it involves biological processes operating at the molecular level of our cells. All healing, no matter how it occurs, has God as its source.

But as much as I appreciate some of his insights, I am bothered by the big picture of Oord's position. For instance, I am not fond of his premise that God is frustrated about things he wants to do, but cannot, because humans aren't cooperating with him.

Also, I disagree with Oord's claim that suffering is never part of God's will in a believer's life. Especially when some very substantial undeserved suffering on a Roman cross is at the heart of the Christian Gospel message. Besides, the Apostle Peter directly contradicts Oord's notion with the following exhortation to some friends who were enduring severe trials: *"Therefore, those also who suffer according to the will of God are to entrust their souls to a faithful Creator in doing what is right"* (1 Peter 4:19, NASB). It could not be any clearer.

Overall, I am troubled by this perspective among some contemporary theologians, Oord being one of them, that God requires humans to come to his defence. They have this idea that his image needs to be cleaned up from its messy medieval past so that he will be more believable, more palatable to modern tastes.

Job himself, at one point in the debate, accuses his friends of doing this very thing: *"Are you defending God with lies? Do you make your dishonest arguments for his sake?"* (Job 13:7) Based on everything he knows about his situation—his relationship with God and his upright character—Job is convinced that his friends are defending God with false statements.

The friends cannot handle the concept of a good God allowing a righteous person to suffer to the degree they see before their eyes, so they believe they must protect God's reputation by presenting him to the world as fairer and more humane than Job is making him out to be.

Like Job's friends, I hear Oord saying, "I'm only going to believe in a God that I can handle in my brain. I will only commit to a divine sovereign who makes sense to me according to my best human reasoning."

In my opinion, this is a dangerous stance to take, for it attempts to eliminate all that is puzzling in the story. I find it arrogant that Oord is unwilling to tolerate any mystery within the nature and work of God, for the Book of Job prompts a lot of mind-boggling thought.

And as I will continue to suggest, the remedy for our human confusion lies in the realm of enlarging our perception of God, not diminishing it.

But be warned: such an exercise isn't easy. It will take great effort to resist the temptation to understand God as merely a very nice human instead of the colossal and magnificent figure he truly is.

However, as we endeavour to figure out the God side of Job's predicament, we must never fail to listen closely to the human side. We need to pay careful attention to what Job says; for if we don't, we run the risk of relegating this important story to the realm of the theoretical, especially if we ourselves have not yet faced exceptionally deep suffering in our lives.

Job is our human representative in this tale, in the real-life enactment of this challenging question of human existence. We must hear all his words—his pain, his sorrow, his complaints, and even his questions—because in the end, God says that Job spoke rightly about him.

So instead of being quick to celebrate only Job's high points of faith, we need to hear everything he has to say. These are the words of a man who is suffering intensely. We need to lean in and allow his sorrow to spill over our souls as he speaks. Listen carefully, not just with your ears, but with your heart.

> *And now my life seeps away.*
>   *Depression haunts my days.*
> *At night my bones are filled with pain,*
>   *which gnaws at me relentlessly.*
> *With a strong hand, God grabs my shirt.*
>   *He grips me by the collar of my coat.*
> *He has thrown me into the mud.*
>   *I'm nothing more than dust and ashes.*

I cry to you, O God, but you don't answer.
    I stand before you, but you don't even look.
You have become cruel toward me.
    You use your power to persecute me.
You throw me into the whirlwind
    and destroy me in the storm.
And I know you are sending me to my death—
    the destination of all who live.

Surely no one would turn against the needy
    when they cry for help in their trouble.
Did I not weep for those in trouble?
    Was I not deeply grieved for the needy?
So I looked for good, but evil came instead.
    I waited for the light, but darkness fell.
My heart is troubled and restless.
    Days of suffering torment me.
I walk in gloom, without sunlight.
    I stand in the public square and cry for help.
Instead, I am considered a brother to jackals
    and a companion to owls.
My skin has turned dark,
    and my bones burn with fever.
My harp plays sad music,
    and my flute accompanies those who weep.
                                     —Job 30:16–31

The Book of Job is real and raw. And there's not much value in glossing over it swiftly for some theological quick hitters. No, it is a piece of inspired literature that needs to be examined carefully and prayerfully to glean a wiser and wider perspective on faith, the nature of God, and man's relationship with God and others in the midst of suffering.

WHAT'S IN IT FOR ME?

Most people who explore the age-old problem of evil want to end up with something useful to say, especially to a friend or family member who's having a rough go of it. But it's tricky when someone appears to have unmerited suffering. How do we handle the dilemma of a godly person walking faithfully with the Lord who experiences suffering out of proportion to their need of correction? What can we say that's helpful?

Sometimes there is no hidden sin to be exposed and confessed. Sometimes the gravity of the misery completely outweighs the potential for character building, particularly for events like genocides and holocausts. Sometimes the person seems to gain no encounter with God throughout the ordeal. God appears to be silent in the face of their horrific and prolonged agony.

For centuries, theologians have tried to come up with a suitable response to this psychological dilemma, something to help calm the hearts of confused and suffering saints.

As discussed, Thomas Jay Oord's position is that God cannot singlehandedly prevent all the evil that happens in the world. According to Oord, God feels our pain, works with others to bring about healing, and attempts to squeeze good out of evil, but he doesn't sovereignly manage the evil himself as part of his plan.

Unsurprisingly, I consider his overall premise to be weak and his thesis wrong. Keeping in step with many other modern theologians,

Oord refuses to believe in or worship a God he can't wrap his head around. He will only bow down to a God he can fully understand, one who makes perfect sense to him intellectually and experientially. In other words, a God who is a lot like him, only better.

I can't help but wonder what Oord thinks when he reads the Book of Job. It's tough to buy into Oord's notion that all evil is out of God's control when God is the one with all the permission-granting power in the story. Satan is at God's mercy in the Book of Job. He can do only what God allows. Accordingly, we need to become comfortable with embracing the mysterious, for Job is a book that spawns a great deal of enigmatic reflection.

Clearly, Job is the classic example of a godly person with unwarranted suffering. The first verse of the book reveals that Job is a man who is *"blameless, upright, fearing God and turning away from evil"* (Job 1:1, NASB). He even acts as a priest for his children, regularly offering sacrifices for each of them after they feast together, asking God to forgive them of sins they might have committed while partying (Job 1:4–5).

God himself testifies to Satan that Job is top-shelf spiritually: *"For there is no one like him on the earth…"* (Job 1:8, NASB) Consequently, the affliction this man endures doesn't appear to be corrective or punitive in nature. So what's the deal?

Whatever else the Book of Job is about, it is most definitely a story concerning pure faith and true religion. It is a tale of spiritual motivation and potential breaking points. Many interpreters see Satan's opening question for God as the key issue of the book: *"Does Job fear God for nothing?"* (Job 1:9, NASB)

Here is the starting point in the discussion, the nerve of the entire drama. Is Job pious toward God only in exchange for privileges? What is the true motivation of his religion?

For that matter, what is the impetus for any believer's faith? Do professing Christians serve God because he is God or because of what he can give them in the bargain? Do they worship God because of what they can get out of it or for what they can become through it?

Certainly, many self-proclaimed Christians practice a form of religion for reasons other than "to glorify God, and to enjoy him forever," as the Westminster Catechism states.[7] Historically in North America, certain social benefits have accompanied church membership, including economic advantages, respectability in the community, and a secure sense of belonging.

Contemporary life in the West is now challenging these past incentives for religious behaviour. Secularism has eroded the economic and social advantages of being a member of a local church. As an institution in the West, the church has not effectively met the physical, social, and emotional needs of many seekers. Nor has it been able to ward off the political, intellectual, and sexual influences of Marx, Nietzsche, and Freud. Prosperity preachers have prostituted the Gospel for their own gain, and more and more theologians favour a discipleship that is less and less costly. Governments have begun to target Christian organizations regarding grant allocations and tax-free non-profit status. Like many of their oppressed Christian brothers and sisters overseas, believers in North America may soon experience multiple levels of persecution for their faith and their views on social matters and identity politics.

The Western world increasingly sees every follower of Christ as a bigoted hater, part of a dying patriarchal value system that has oppressed its victims for too long—women, racial minorities, LGBTQ+ community, etc. As has been the case in many other countries, Christianity in the West is undergoing a shakedown that will reduce religion to its purest motivation. When things get rough and all earthly benefits for the Christian faith are gone, will believers still be willing to serve God just because he is God?

---

[7] "Westminster Catechism," *Britannica*. Date of access: July 12, 2021 (https://www.britannica.com/topic/Westminster-Catechism).

Job's drama begs the question: is there a faith in God that is real and independent of our affluence or poverty, not threatened by our pleasure or pain? Job's response to the upcoming firestorm will provide the answer.

Satan lays out his position on the matter clearly:

Job has good reason to fear God. You have always put a wall of protection around him and his home and his property. You have made him prosper in everything he does. Look how rich he is! But reach out and take away everything he has, and he will surely curse you to your face!

—Job 1:9–11

It's fascinating to see that God wastes no time in taking up the adversary's challenge. Why? Because Satan's insinuation belittles both God and humanity. If Satan is correct—if the motive of God's servant is selfish, and if God must bribe humans to worship him—the very foundation of a true love relationship between God and man is destroyed. If God must dangle rewards in front of people to entice them to spirituality, then he is manipulative. If man's goodness stems from a contract to ward off trouble, piety becomes hypocrisy.

Satan's charge is profoundly serious. Such a devastating accusation could not go unanswered. Divine and human reputations alike are at stake.

Yet Job knew nothing of this heavenly discussion. Without his awareness, Job was selected by God to refute the slanderer, to silence Satan. Can he do it?

As the drama begins, Job's charge out of the starting blocks is remarkable. In response to hearing the devastating news of the sudden and total loss of his possessions, servants, and children,

> *Job stood up and tore his robe in grief. Then he shaved his head and fell to the ground to worship. He said, "I came naked from my mother's womb, and I will be naked when I leave. The Lord gave me what I had, and the Lord has taken it away. Praise the name of the Lord!" In all of this, Job did not sin by blaming God.*
>
> —Job 1:20–21

Job passes the first part of the test with a solid A+. His religion is instantly purged of any superficial or selfish motivation. His opening response reveals the possibility of a faith whose value lies in the personal relationship it creates rather than the benefits that come from it. He humbly submits himself to God's sovereignty, expressing gratitude to the Creator for what he has enjoyed up until the present. Most striking in Job's response is his posture of reverence for the Lord, a reverence based on the truth that God alone is worthy of all praise, honour, and glory.

The revelation of this truth is so important that God is willing to subject his prize servant to grief and poverty to make it known. And as Job arises and speaks these incredible words of faith, Satan is proved wrong. The superior worth of God becomes evident to all.

So Job survives the initial onslaught. Theologically, he's somewhat thriving. But the real question becomes, can he hang on? For this is just the beginning. Job is headed for an even darker realm of doom, a valley of unspeakable agony.

Job has shown that God is more valuable to him than family and possessions. But what about his health? Will Job still treasure God over good health?

To find the answer, God hands Job over to Satan for the destruction of his flesh. Here's where we enter some nasty territory, terrain where memorized theological explanations fail to fit the experience, where best friends let you down, and where suffering far surpasses any cause or lesson that could be learned from it. This is territory where the meaning of life itself hangs in the balance.

We pick up the drama again in Job 2:1.

> *One day the members of the heavenly court came again to present themselves before the Lord, and the Accuser, Satan, came with them. "Where have you come from?" the Lord asked Satan.*
>
> *Satan answered the Lord, "I have been patrolling the earth, watching everything that's going on."*
>
> *Then the Lord asked Satan, "Have you noticed my servant Job? He is the finest man in all the earth. He is blameless—a man of complete integrity. He fears God and stays away from evil. And he has maintained his integrity, even though you urged me to harm him without cause."*
>
> *Satan replied to the Lord, "Skin for skin! A man will give up everything he has to save his life. But reach out and take away his health, and he will surely curse you to your face!"*
>
> *"All right, do with him as you please," the Lord said to Satan. "But spare his life." So Satan left the Lord's presence, and he struck Job with terrible boils from head to foot.*
>
> *Job scraped his skin with a piece of broken pottery as he sat among the ashes. His wife said to him, "Are you still trying to maintain your integrity? Curse God and die."*
>
> *But Job replied, "You talk like a foolish woman. Should we accept only good things from the hand of God and never anything bad?" So in all this, Job said nothing wrong.*
>
> —Job 2:1–10

Considering the physiological gravity of this debilitation, on the heels of the horrific loss of everything he held dear, Job's response is astounding. Many people curse God on the day of their calamity, yet few ever suffer this level of adversity, wave upon wave. A lesser man might have sarcastically bellowed, "Oh, nice! This is how you reward me, God, for worshipping you reverently after the loss of my family and my wealth? I did it right and so you whack me again? Thanks a lot!"

But no such words come out of Job's mouth. Suffering excruciatingly with boils from head to toe, he maintains his integrity and reverence for God.

I have never had a boil, but my wife has. Two, in fact. And I saw how painful they were for her. The one on the back of her leg completely incapacitated her. She couldn't even walk. I guess that's why Job just sat there in the heap of ashes, scraping himself with a piece of broken pottery.

As far as Job's wife is concerned… well, it's all too much for her. She has endured with him the loss of their children and wealth. But now with the life of her husband draining away, her faith collapses. She tells Job to curse God and die, perhaps causing a hopeful smile to cross Satan's face.

But Job's faith bursts through in glorious victory like the morning sun shattering the haziness of dawn: *"Should we accept only good things from the hand of God and never anything bad?"* (Job 2:10) Job fully believes that human comforts and calamities come equally from the hand of God. And this faithful servant will not relinquish his confidence in the benevolent sovereignty of God, regardless of the calamity that assails him.

Job's response brings fuller meaning to the words of the Apostle Peter, recorded in one of his letters written to persecuted churches in New Testament times:

> *Your adversary the devil prowls around like a roaring lion, seeking someone to devour. Resist him, firm in your faith, knowing that the same kinds of suffering are being experienced by your brotherhood throughout the world.*
>
> —1 Peter 5:8–9, ESV

Peter makes an astute connection between Christian suffering and the work of Satan. Yes, the devil wants to hurt Christians. This intention makes the evil one an adversary.

But believers resist him most effectively and curb his negative influence in their lives by remaining steadfast in their faith. Like Job, suffering believers need to place their confidence in the sovereign goodness of God. They must resist the natural urge to curse him, and then hunt hard for ways to revere him. When devoted followers demonstrate that kind of trust in the Lord, Satan is defeated.

Instead of clamouring for precise answers and then becoming angry or bitter when they don't materialize, believers best respond to their suffering by mimicking Job, throwing themselves at the feet of God in total submission to his providential care. The Apostle Peter gave that same advice to suffering believers who were in his spiritual care: *"Therefore, those also who suffer according to the will of God are to entrust their souls to a faithful Creator in doing what is right"* (1 Peter 4:19, NASB).

As we proceed through the Book of Job, we will have front row seats to witness this true follower of Yahweh entrusting his soul to the Creator. Certainly, Job's ordeal will not come without some challenging questions, but he never abandons his relationship with God. And that, as we will see, makes all the difference.

A person's initial response to tragedy says a lot about their character, where their heart is at. And first impressions are lasting impressions. Job's immediate response of faith to the concentric waves of calamity afflicting him burns its way into our psyche forever. No blame. Just holy reverence for an almighty, all-loving God. Job declares, *"Praise the name of the Lord!"* (Job 1:21) This humble posture is a far cry from typical human responses to tragedy.

Job knew the truth from the very beginning—life is really about the giver of life. It's not about what we think we deserve or don't deserve. It's about God and having faith in that God as one who is worthy of our praise and adoration just because of who he is, not because of something we think he is going to give us in return.

Job reveals that his default mode is an intrinsic willingness to love and serve God regardless of his current state of personal comfort. Satan's question is answered, but not in the way he predicted.

Is there a faith in God that is real, independent of our affluence or poverty, and unthreatened by our pleasure or pain? Apparently, there is. And thereby comes the challenge to all who profess to be followers of Christ: are you also willing to surrender totally to God and serve him for nothing, for no guaranteed earthly benefit or payoff?

WHOSE FIGHT IS THIS ANYWAY?

Before advancing the narrative further, it would be wise to pause and ponder the true nature of the conflict in this ancient drama. Can we identify the opponents? Is this a God versus Job scenario? Is it Satan versus Job? Or is it God versus Satan? Though Job is more inclined to see it as a scuffle between himself and God, the first two chapters of the text seem to indicate the primacy of the last option. This is a battle principally between God and Satan.

This great battle concerns the viability of a pure relationship between God and the pinnacle of his creation. Does God need to bribe people to love and serve him? Do humans behave well only because they think God will recompense them for their trouble? Or is the sovereign Lord worth worshipping just because of who he is?

When anyone broaches the subject of who God is, they are compelled to discuss the greatness of his incredible glory. And the first order of business is to ask, what does God himself say about the topic? How does he handle the subject of his glory?

We at times joke tongue-in-cheek about the concept of greatness. *It's hard to be humble when you're so great!* But for God, ironically, this is the only approach he can take. If he is who he says he is, his glory must take pre-eminence in every scenario of life, for there is nothing more valuable than shining the entire spotlight on the majesty and magnificence of the one who formed and sustains all creation.

Both the Old and New Testament are inundated with hundreds of references to God's glory in all aspects of creation. The all-time classic in Psalm 19:1 declares, *"The heavens proclaim the glory of God."* Truly, an upward gaze on a starry night prompts a response of wonder and amazement at God's infinite majesty.

But the Scriptures also make reference to God's glory in many other facets of life. Examples include the overwhelming glory experienced by humans when God makes his presence tangibly known (like Moses on Mount Sinai or the Jewish faithful during the dedication of Solomon's temple), the glory of God involved in Christ's miraculous ministry (John 11:4), the powerful glory associated with Christ's establishment of his eternal Kingdom (Luke 21:27), the glory God receives when an individual confesses Jesus to be their Lord (Philippians 2:11), and most importantly the command to do everything in life with the purpose of glorifying the Creator: *"So whether you eat or drink, or whatever you do, do it all for the glory of God"* (1 Corinthians 10:31).

In fact, if you were to attempt to single out a unifying theme of the entire Bible, it could easily be the glory of God. But finding the word glory and its derivatives in the text is certainly easier than defining the term itself. The glory of God is referenced everywhere in Scripture, but what does it mean?

God's glory could be described as his brilliance, his radiant beauty, his high honour, his greatness, his majesty, or his praiseworthiness. For God to be glorified, he must be shown to be as wonderful and terrifying as the Creator of everything needs to be. Some theologians, like John Piper, have defined God's glory as "the manifest beauty of his holiness."[8] In colloquial terms, we would probably use the word *awesome*. Regardless of how we try to describe it, if we

---

[8] "What is God's Glory," *Desiring God*. Date of access: July 16, 2020 (https://www.desiringgod.org/interviews/what-is-gods-glory--2).

saw God's glory in its fullness, we would recognize it most definitely, provided we survive the experience.

Now, when the God of the Bible talks about his glory, he says some fascinating things. To a believer, God's proclamations ring true. But some of the Almighty's claims have a controversial feel for critics and skeptics.

One of the great Hebrew prophets of old records the following proclamation made by Yahweh: *"I am the Lord; that is my name! I will not give my glory to anyone else, nor share my praise with carved idols"* (Isaiah 42:8).

God is protective of his glory and demands that humans esteem it appropriately. When agnostics or atheists come upon such statements in Scripture, they are quick to accuse Yahweh of being an egotistical, self-centred megalomaniac. They find his glory-seeking offensive.

But such negative responses arise only because of a faulty notion regrettably present within the human imagination—namely, an exaggerated comfort level with envisioning God as just a really good human. The thinking usually goes something like this: "A very nice person would never seek their own attention and glory all the time. So, if I as a pretty good person would never act this way, God must surely behave better than me, and never, ever act this way."

However, to explain the nature of God in this manner reveals that the thinker is subconsciously picturing God as the best possible human one can imagine. Putting God on the same continuum as humans, these critics envision the Lord as standing exceptionally high up the ladder on the human decency scale. Because respectable humans behave in such a fine manner in certain circumstances, God should behave in an extremely good version of that manner in those same circumstances.

If God were merely an exceptional human, this logic would be fair and just. But he is not the best human we can imagine. He is the God who made all the humans, even the really good ones we happen to know. Consequently, all that is amazing and fantastic about him needs to be displayed wherever and whenever possible. When that fails to happen, a deficit is present in the situation.

The ultimate target to which a human can shoot is God's glory. We are to worship and adore it by striving to glorify him through every morsel of behavior we can muster. *"For everything comes from him and exists by his power and is intended for his glory"* (Romans 11:36). Because of his divine nature and unmatched character, showcasing God's glory is the greatest goal in all history—past, present, and future. If God promoted any other objective within his creation, he would be acting in contradiction with his utmost pre-eminence.

In today's vernacular, God is so great that if he doesn't blow his own horn, he's doing it wrong. When something—or in this case, someone—is recognized as being supreme in every category imaginable, to deprive them of the gold medal wouldn't just be shameful, it would be an utter disaster.

Even though human metaphors can't fully capture the essence of God's glory, he is committed to preserving it.

And in the story of Job, that's what God is doing. His battle with Satan is to defend his glory. Is the sovereign Lord as great as he claims? Is he worth our worship and faithful devotion, even when every temporal blessing is withdrawn?

In this ancient tale, God makes himself and his reputation vulnerable by leaving it up to his faithful servant to deliver the goods. Only if Job can stay the course in the cesspool of suffering will God be properly glorified in his servant's life. Only if Job refuses to abandon God will the Lord be shown publicly to be worthy of undivided worship in every possible circumstance of human life, good or bad.

With that in mind, consider four theological truths that stem from the fact that the true battle in this story is between God and

Satan. John Piper highlighted these truths in a sermon several decades ago.[9]

The first theological truth is no surprise. In every facet of life, Satan aims to destroy the joy of God in the life of Christian believers. Our great adversary uses two weapons to achieve this task: pain and pleasure. Satan uses pain to make us feel that God is powerless or hostile. He uses pleasure to make us feel that God is unnecessary.

The adversary failed to turn Job away from God in the days of his pleasure and prosperity, so he attacked Job's God-centred joy through pain, only to fail again.

Clearly, there can be no doubt about what Satan is after in the lives of those who faithfully try to follow the Lord. His aim is to destroy a believer's joy in God and to replace the treasure of the Almighty with the earthly treasures of health, wealth, and family.

Secondly, God aims to magnify his worth in the lives of his followers. The great purpose of God in creation and redemption is to preserve and display the infinite worth of his glory. He does this by redeeming the people who love and cleave to him, cherishing him above all earthly treasures and pleasures. The mirror he has chosen for the reflection of his worth is the indestructible joy of his people. Faithful followers of Christ honour God best when they will not trade him for anything this world has to offer.

In the New Testament, the Apostle Paul expands on this concept by sharing his outlook on the goal of Christian persecution. When Paul experienced hardship for faithfully following the Lord, his sole desire was to have the glorious life of Jesus reflected in his response to the suffering.

> *Through suffering, our bodies continue to share in the death of Jesus so that the life of Jesus may also be seen in our bodies.*

---

[9] "Job: Reverent in Suffering," *Desiring God*. Date of access: July 16, 2020 (https://www.desiringgod.org/messages/job-reverent-in-suffering).

> *Yes, we live under constant danger of death because we serve Jesus, so that the life of Jesus will be evident in our dying bodies.*
> —2 Corinthians 4:10–11

The greatest suffering saint of the New Testament agrees with his Old Testament counterpart—through sunshine and rain, all that matters in life is the glory of God.

Thirdly, as God and Satan do battle, God grants to Satan limited power to cause pain in the lives of humans. As the text shows, God sets the limits of Satan's power to inflict pain.

In contrast to Thomas Oord's perspective, God is not frustrated by the power and subtlety of Satan. Satan cannot make a move without the permission of God Almighty. Satan may be a lion, but he's a lion on a leash. And God reins him in or gives him slack according to his own sovereign purposes.

And finally, Satan's work in this world is ultimately the work of God. In the two heavenly scenes described in the account, God hands Job over to Satan's power. But in both cases, when Satan has done his dirty deeds, Job ascribes the tragedies to be within the realm of God's sovereignty. Job declares that the Lord himself has ultimately taken away his family, his wealth, and his health.

> *The Lord gave me what I had, and the Lord has taken it away.*
> —Job 1:21

> *Should we accept only good things from the hand of God and never anything bad?*
> —Job 2:10

And in both rounds of the assault, the inspired writer of the book declares that there was no sin in what Job said.

> *In all of this, Job did not sin by blaming God.*
>
> —Job 1:22

> *So in all this, Job said nothing wrong.*
>
> —Job 2:10

At first, we might be thrown by the idea of Job ascribing to God what Satan had clearly done. But truly, this whole scene plays out as a bold declaration of the absolute certainty of God's sovereignty. Even when Satan works, God is at work.

This principle is evident elsewhere in Scripture. When Joseph was hurled into years of tumultuous and unjust suffering, the summary delivered to his deceptive and no doubt satanically inspired brothers sums it up rightly:

> *But don't be upset, and don't be angry with yourselves for selling me to this place. It was God who sent me here ahead of you to preserve your lives… God has sent me ahead of you to keep you and your families alive and to preserve many survivors. So it was God who sent me here, not you! And he is the one who made me an adviser to Pharaoh—the manager of his entire palace and the governor of all Egypt.*
>
> —Genesis 45:5, 7–8

Later, when his father Jacob died and the brothers feared repercussions finally arriving from the hand of their younger brother, Joseph reassured them that he wasn't out for vengeance. Understanding the mystery of the sovereignty of God, he said to them, *"You intended to harm me, but God intended it all for good"* (Genesis 50:20).

When Satan works, God is at work.

In the New Testament, we don't need to look any further than the crucifixion of Christ to see this truth in full operation. As Satan was working in the heart of Judas to betray his Lord, and then in the hearts of the Jewish leadership to push for Christ's execution, God was ultimately working out his plan of salvation for the world.

When Satan works, God is at work.

Even the final book of the Bible speaks of Christian saints overcoming Satan by remaining fearless in the face of martyrdom (Revelation 12:11).

To this day, as the great enemy of God's people schemes to torture and murder followers of Christ, the devil creates his own demise by encouraging the very thing that will eventually conquer him. God will use the faithful endurance and testimony of his people amidst tribulation to defeat their great enemy once and for all.

And because it is God's power that enables his children to remain faithful, the Lord will receive all the glory he deserves in the end.

You see, the big struggle has always been between God and Satan, and God's definition of victory is the triumph of his glory permeating all of creation. Believers must continually point their compass toward the prioritization and celebration of the glory of God.

Satan perpetually works against that goal, but he will eventually lose the entire war, just like he loses in the story of Job. And Satan loses because his foe isn't just a somewhat energetic being who resembles a really good human with very nice intentions. No, Satan loses because his opponent is the all-powerful, all-knowing, all-present Lord of the universe, the very one who will quietly and mightily come alongside Job and carry him through his deepest and darkest valley.

QUESTIONS FOR GOD

Round One

Any time we crack open the Old Testament and peruse the story of Job, we are obliged to discuss the age-old problem of evil and suffering in our world. How can a benevolent loving God who is all-powerful allow bad things to happen to good people? This confounding riddle disrupts our human sense of justice and assaults our sentiment. When tragic events arrive unexpectedly in our own lives, or in the lives of those we love, we convince ourselves that a moral violation has occurred.

As humans, we persistently look for patterns of causality. We are meaning-makers. We want to be assured that we live in a stable, orderly world. But beyond trying to make the world precise and predictable, we very much want to believe that the world is fair, that people get what they deserve.

For our own peace of mind, we need our world to make sense. It's easier to sleep at night when we hold a signed contract guaranteeing that on this planet everything happens for a reason—not just natural reasons (it rained because a low-pressure system moved in over us), but moral reasons (it rained because we are good, honest people and we prayed for it).

And when we speak of moral causes for the circumstances of life, we are inevitably invoking not just Creator God, but a virtuous God who we believe rewards goodness and punishes evil.

As the story reveals, Job's friends are comfortable in a meaning-maker paradigm with oversimplified moral declarations. They desperately want to assure themselves that Job's suffering is justified. They cannot handle the thought of living in a world where God might allow a righteous man to suffer for no apparent reason.

Theologians attempt to explain this conundrum by latching on to one of two approaches; either they imagine God to be smaller and less in control of world events and people's personal affairs, or they strive to make him bigger and even more mysterious than the average person desires him to be. Those who favour a smaller concept of God believe they are helping him out by making him more intelligible, more lovable—dare I say, more human—because he simply cannot control all the evil things that inevitably happen in a fallen world. In other words, "Don't be mad at God for your tragedy. He loves you but couldn't prevent the evil from happening because there is free will in the world."

The Book of Job, however, leans more toward the second approach. In this story, God is very big.

But from Job's perspective, the sovereign rule of this big God isn't easily understood. Blending his sovereignty with his goodness is mysterious, and the dialogue between Job and his friends tracks the struggle of trying to sort out the kind of world we really live in. Are there patterns and formulas for producing the healthy and fruitful life we all desire, or can life end up looking more random and chaotic than we want to admit?

Without warning, indescribably horrible things happen to the most righteous man on the planet. Yet Job's initial response is astounding. He refuses to curse God for the loss of all his wealth, children, and health. His confession demonstrates a strong resolve to serve God for nothing.

In the presence of God, Satan had accused Job of being devoted to the Almighty only for the material benefits. But Job's opening reaction proves the accuser wrong. Humans *can* possess a faith in God that is real, independent of affluence or poverty, and unthreatened by pleasure or pain.

But enter the great tester of the human soul—time. Sometimes seasoned faith carries a person through the first waves of sorrow. Sometimes it's adrenaline. But when the suffering is prolonged, time has a way of wearing people down.

How long did Job suffer? We don't know for sure, but there are some hints in the text. In Job 7:3, he refers to himself as being assigned *"months of futility."* In Job 14:14, he says that if he was guaranteed a good afterlife, that would provide him some hope in *"all my years of struggle."* So we can be certain that this was not just a few days or weeks of suffering. This was a long ordeal.

As we have seen, Job could handle the load at first. But then, sitting in that ash heap day after day, the horror of his condition sinks in. All he has now are his thoughts and his pain. With no hope in sight, he begins to unravel. This isn't how God is supposed to operate in this world. Job's angst leads to a great deal of complaining and questions. Questions for God, and even some that sound rather angry.

If you take the time to scrutinize Job's speeches, you may be surprised to discover what Job says to God. He doesn't hold back. He is far more perturbed than patient. And speaking of patience, when the New Testament writer James references Job, he celebrates his perseverance or steadfastness, not so much his patience (James 5:11). This popular concept of the patience of Job has taken root in the subconscious because of the King James Version's mistranslation of the Greek word in the text, which literally means *endurance* rather than *patience*. Job endures. He perseveres. He hangs in there. He is more steadfast than patient.

But by the end of the story, God declares that it was Job who spoke rightly of him, not his friends. We need to keep this in mind as we go through the dialogue. Our challenge will be to discern what

Job did right in all his complaining, and what his friends did wrong by merely reciting their theological textbook of supposed truth.

Indeed, it's a puzzler. The friends do nothing but defend God and talk nicely about him while Job is, at times, patently upset with God. Truly, how is it that the friends are sinning and Job is not?

Though we may not yet fully understand the answer to this question, I think we are safe in assuming that God is okay with hurting and frustrated believers expressing their emotions to him, even if those emotions include anger. God allows Job to be honest. Asking God tough questions is okay.

Because God can handle tough questions, let us devote some space to examine the three that really bothered Job the most:

1. How do we find meaning in life when things go bad?
2. Why does God seem so silent in our darkest hour?
3. Why do the wicked so often prosper in this life?

As we examine these questions over the next three chapters, you may find yourself easily identifying with this Old Testament saint. Perhaps you'll recall asking these very same questions at one time or another. Perhaps you're asking them right now. Don't be surprised if you find this centuries-old text to be very relevant to your own world.

To start this journey of human questioning, let us consider perhaps the most prevalent theme in Job's speeches—namely, the question of searching for meaning when life has totally fallen apart. Amidst gut-wrenching tragedy, it's easy to question the ultimate purpose of one's existence. When personal situations deteriorate savagely, what is the point of even being alive?

After seven days of sitting in silence with his friends, Job finally lost his composure and *"cursed the day of his birth"* (Job 3:1). Reading through the verses that follow, we hear a poetic outcry resembling the lament of the prophet Jeremiah when he was at his lowest point of despair.

> *Let the day of my birth be erased,*
> *   and the night I was conceived.*
> *Let that day be turned to darkness…*
> *Let that night be blotted off the calendar…*
> *Curse that day for failing to shut my mother's womb,*
> *   for letting me be born to see all this trouble.*
>
> *Why wasn't I born dead?*
> *   Why didn't I die as I came from the womb?…*
> *Had I died at birth, I would now be at peace.*
> *   I would be asleep and at rest…*
> *Why wasn't I buried like a stillborn child,*
> *   like a baby who never lives to see the light?*
>
> —Job 3:3–4, 6, 10–11, 13, 16

Job asks God what many suffering people ask: *"Oh, why give light to those in misery, and life to those who are bitter?… Why is life given to those with no future, those God has surrounded with difficulties?"* (Job 3:20, 23) In today's vernacular, "What is the point of being alive when your life totally sucks?"

Some people may be quick to stand up and respond. Those currently enjoying good health, delightful relationships, and a decent measure of wealth might criticize such a seemingly offensive and faithless question. When things are going well for a believer, the meaning of life seems obvious—to glorify God and serve him in his Kingdom. Such a believer thinks, *Sure, we all face trials sometimes, but we must see these challenges as opportunities for character development.*

The Sunday school answer seems easy when one isn't in deep and prolonged pain. But when loss upon loss mounts up and the suffering reaches unbearable levels, life's purpose begins to blur. Instead of hopeful sentiments for a better future, the aching heart may only be able to summon a cry to end it all.

Job gets it. He's right there.

> *Oh, that I might have my request,*
>   *that God would grant my desire.*
> *I wish he would crush me.*
>   *I wish he would reach out his hand and kill me.*
> *At least I can take comfort in this:*
>   *Despite the pain,*
>   *I have not denied the words of the Holy One.*
> *But I don't have the strength to endure.*
>   *I have nothing to live for.*
>
> —Job 6:8–11

Not only did he wish he had never been born, or even conceived, he wanted God to take him out. He wanted to die. In his words, *"I have nothing to live for."*

Back in the 1980s, my wife and I lived in a small town in southern Ontario. We made many good friends in that town, including a fine young couple I will refer to as Grant and Gloria. They were in their twenties when they became Christians and began to attend our church. They were a beautiful family with two nice kids, a girl and a boy. Grant, a handsome man, was an engineer at a nearby power plant. Gloria was the perfect homemaker and host of many entertaining galas. Jeanette and I always had a wonderful time in their quaint, warm home. Despite no Christian family support in their heritage, Grant and Gloria remained steady and faithful followers of Jesus.

Then, in 1987, Gloria got shingles. Shingles victims often emerge from their ordeal relatively unscathed, and so the gravity of the situation wasn't initially apparent.

Gloria was not so lucky. While many get shingles on their back or legs, she got the infection on her face. The disease did extensive and irreparable damage to the nerves in her head. And then, on the heels of that ordeal, she was diagnosed with multiple sclerosis. The combination of these two health issues ended up totally incapacitating this once vibrant and flourishing young woman.

To make a long story short, for the past three decades of her life Gloria has lived with excruciating head pain that regularly causes her to throw up. She spends nearly every day of her life in bed in great discomfort, with no relief in sight. Medication has done next to nothing to relieve her suffering.

To add insult to injury, Grant, her primary caregiver, is bipolar, and his condition has deteriorated under the stress of her suffering.

Amazingly, Gloria has maintained her faith in God. But from her physical and psychological standpoint, she has very little to live for in this world. Like Job, she has at times wished that God would just kill her.

I don't blame her. I have never experienced anything close to her level of pain. I've had broken bones, severely cut myself on occasion, and dislocated my shoulder numerous times, but I've never suffered any extended adversity. I once had a strain of Asian flu that lasted two weeks, and the medication I took improperly damaged the lining of my stomach. The pain I experienced in that adventure was severe. At the time, it seemed like my suffering was never going to end. But as much as I might have thought I was going to die, I eventually recovered.

Pain does strange things to the brain. It's tough to think about anything else when you're in the middle of such agony. It has a way of driving us into a singularity of thought. When we hurt, it's hard to imagine ever feeling good again; it can be difficult to remember what it was like to not feel pain.

No wonder Job says at one point, *"I will never again feel happiness"* (Job 7:7).

Besides the angst of the moment, prolonged suffering can permanently damage a healthy brain, causing depression, anxiety, memory loss, and concentration struggles, making rational assessments and social interactions much more difficult.

Some of Job's comments reflect this. When he was healthy, I doubt Job would make this type of allegation:

> *I despise my life.*
> *Innocent or wicked, it is all the same to God.*
> > *That's why I say, "He destroys both the blameless and*
> > *the wicked."*
> *When a plague sweeps through,*
> > *he laughs at the death of the innocent.*
>
> —Job 9:21–23

Being a virtuous man of integrity, it's doubtful Job really believed God mockingly laughs at innocent people dying. The man was a bit out of his mind.

For another case in point, consider the rant where Job accuses God of duplicity:

> *You formed me with your hands; you made me,*
> > *yet now you completely destroy me.*
> *Remember that you made me from dust—*
> > *will you turn me back to dust so soon?*
> *You guided my conception*
> > *and formed me in the womb.*
> *You clothed me with skin and flesh,*
> > *and you knit my bones and sinews together.*

You gave me life and showed me your unfailing love.
  My life was preserved by your care.

Yet your real motive—
  your true intent—
was to watch me, and if I sinned,
  you would not forgive my guilt.

—Job 10:8–14

After a lyrical description of God's miraculous sovereignty in the process of human gestation, Job concludes that the Almighty's overriding purpose has been just to catch him sinning, and then cruelly punish him indefinitely.

Again, he's not in his right mind because of the pain.

Besides the biological effects on the brain caused by extensive physical and psychological agony, Job also lacked the eschatological insights possessed by those now operating on the other side of the New Testament. Job didn't know much, if anything, about the resurrection. Listen to his pessimistic perception of the afterlife:

Even a tree has more hope!
  If it is cut down, it will sprout again
and grow new branches.
Though its roots have grown old in the earth
  and its stump decays,
at the scent of water it will bud
  and sprout again like a new seedling.

But when people die, their strength is gone.
  They breathe their last, and then where are they?
As water evaporates from a lake
  and a river disappears in drought,

> *people are laid to rest and do not rise again.*
> *Until the heavens are no more, they will not wake up*
> *nor be roused from their sleep.*
>
> —Job 14:7–12

In the same passage, he references a glimmer of hope for eternal life, but it's not a certainty for him: *"Can the dead live again? If so, this would give me hope through all my years of struggle, and I would eagerly await the release of death"* (Job 14:14).

Regardless of what Job understands about the afterlife, he cannot find any meaning in his present life. He would simply prefer to die right now. He says, *"I would rather be strangled—rather die than suffer like this. I hate my life and don't want to go on living"* (Job 7:15–16).

When human adversity becomes overwhelming and relief is nowhere in sight, it's easy—and common—for people to conclude that there's no point in living. Protracted suffering drives us to despair, depriving us of purpose for the present or future. Many take their own lives.

My wife had a high school friend whom I'll call Brenda. They were in the same grade and grew up playing sports together. Unfortunately, at the age of nineteen Brenda was diagnosed with rheumatoid arthritis. Her entire adult life went into a downward spiral of crippling and painful physical limitations. Giving birth to a child further exacerbated her symptoms. In time, the pain and debilitation of her arthritis forced her into a wheelchair where she eventually became dependent on others to feed her and meet her basic needs.

In the summer of 2019, Brenda contracted a serious infection in her leg that required amputation. Sizing up her agonizing situation and measuring her feelings of hopelessness, she chose to forego the surgery and end her life. On August 23 of that year, Brenda passed away by assisted suicide. Because she could no longer see any purpose for her life, she wanted to end it all.

Regardless of your philosophical or theological stance on suicide, Brenda's narrative is a very sad story. Unless you yourself have experienced this level of darkness, it's hard to appreciate the angst and despair such a person feels. And there are many people in this world who walk exceedingly sad and painful journeys.

Sometimes chipper followers of Jesus are quick to intervene in sorrowful situations with the intent of correcting negative outlooks. Great is the temptation to fix the faulty worldviews of the Eeyores in their world.

Now, to be fair, Christians who try to encourage the downtrodden by sharing the joys of living for Jesus do so, largely, with sincere motives. At the same time, we cannot downplay what people are feeling when they're in horrible situations. If you've ever endured serious prolonged suffering, you know what I'm talking about. It can be a struggle to find any meaning in life under the weight of oppressive physical and emotional agony.

As uncomfortable and unresolved as it may feel, we need to understand the value of allowing people to express their true feelings amidst tragedy, as opposed to sharing zealously what is believed to be the right answers to their questions. It's always easy to have the right answers when sitting on the other side of suffering.

If your first response to a suffering victim is to remind them that God is sovereign over their painful situation, you should recognize that the statement may be theologically true, but by using it you're also delivering an instant reprimand to that person's emotions. As soon as the clichés arrive, emotional honesty is shut down. Victims are made to feel guilty for continuing to vent after they've already been told the platitudinal good news that God is in control and everything will work out fine.

Curiously, God never instigates any such emotional shutdown in the Book of Job. He doesn't steamroll Job's feelings. He doesn't respond immediately by throwing lightning bolts. Nor does he appear instantly to rebuke Job's anger and despair.

Instead, from the time of the assault on his health, God waits thirty-five chapters before appearing to Job. The suffering saint is given a lot of room to get it out of his system. Job accuses God of being unfair, cries for a hearing, agonizes over his situation, and skates dangerously close to blaspheming God, as Satan hoped he would.

But take note—as the story unfolds, Job is not allowed to stay in that angry place. His harsh words are never encouraged or condoned.

In the interim, God allows him this turbulent space to be authentic. A God worth worshipping is a God who prefers honest emotions over hypocritical praise or flattery any day of the week.

Can a believer be brave enough to be honest with God when things go sideways or spiral downward? When their life goes south, many feel pressured to pretend everything is okay, even in their prayers. Some attempt to show their reverence for God by treating him as a schoolteacher who demands their politeness.

But prayer is not supposed to be a mere recitation of well-behaved words. It is a time of true connection with God. Whatever the circumstance, God can handle the heavy emotions that tough trials tend to produce. He has broad shoulders.

Please hear carefully what I'm saying. When harbouring blame and nursing ongoing anger toward God become a lifestyle, it destroys a person's soul. In the course of time, Job will need to stop his complaining. Elihu will eventually call upon him to repent for speaking bitterly against God.

However, journeys of suffering are exactly that—a journey. And expressions of emotional honesty, particularly in the early phases of grief, play a vital role in the healing process. As well, remembering the fact that God is the architect of human emotions, I am certain they don't scare him.

Sometimes it might be okay to ask God the question: "Given that my life is so horrible right now, what purpose do you still have for me? Can I truly find some meaning in the mess of my current situation?" And if you're a bystander who happens to hear such cries from a fellow traveller, I encourage you to remember that being allowed to ask the right questions in life can often be more valuable and bring more healing than just being told the right answers.

QUESTIONS FOR GOD

Round Two

We all have some level of expectation or, at least, hope as to how God runs the universe. Working off the assumption that he is loving, fair, and just, we want God to keep the moral order of things operating in a way that resonates with our rational minds. We would like to see good works rewarded and wrongdoing punished.

In the Book of Job, our main character also wants the moral system of the universe to function the way he and his friends believe it works—good guys getting blessed, bad guys getting whacked.

Though we haven't yet given our attention to the contributions of Job's companions—Eliphaz, Bildad, and Zophar—they repeatedly remind their suffering friend that the system *is* working just fine. The problem lies with Job. He must be harbouring unconfessed sin in his life. Clearly, they fear it being otherwise. Job alludes to their obvious concern: *"You have seen my calamity, and you are afraid"* (Job 6:21). The friends had to be thinking, *If God doesn't always run the universe in the moral fashion we think, we could be in some serious trouble ourselves. If this level of calamity can happen to righteous Job, what might happen to us?*

But Job's heart is troubled because he isn't sure that this moral universe *is* working right. Even more than the *pain* of his suffering, Job is crushed by the *shock* of his suffering. His situation, coupled with the very common unfettered prosperity of the wicked, leaves him in a state of great confusion. The math doesn't add up. And he's thinking,

If the system doesn't work the way we've always believed it works, then I am in deep despair and I have no reason to live. I want to die.

As we saw earlier, Job's first big question for God concerns how one finds meaning in life when life hurts so badly. As he says, *"I have nothing to live for"* (Job 6:11).

This is a common sentiment among many today, especially in North America. Worldwide, on average, about one out of every ten thousand people take their own life each year, with twenty-five times that number attempting to do so.[10] You never know who's walking in your midst, floundering in a pool of purposelessness. So much internal suffering goes unnoticed.

Eliphaz, Bildad, and Zophar, on the other hand, are completely aware of their friend's fragile state of mind. Job's mental anguish is no secret. He is devastated and repeatedly bellows out his despair.

It is important to let Job question God aggressively and say what he needs to say. Well-intentioned counsellors are far too quick to give what they believe to be the right theological solutions to desperate people's problems.

Unfortunately, hurting people are often denied the chance to express their raw emotions. Under the guise of faith and good Christianity, many of those who suffer don't feel free to divulge their feelings about the horror that has become their life. They may be afraid to be honest with God and their disappointment with him. Such repression of emotions and hypocritical piety aren't healthy, psychologically or spiritually.

God allows Job to be totally honest. Not only is this freedom healthy for Job from a physiological standpoint, it will also expose Job to some darker aspects of his inner man he may not yet have understood. This genuineness provides a measure of strength that will

---

[10] "Suicide Facts," *Suicide Awareness Voices of Education*. Date of access: July 23, 2020 (https://save.org/about-suicide/suicide-facts/).

help Job endure his difficult journey. In time, it will also play a part in his eventual repentance and recovery.

Now, for all his rants and raves, there's something unique about Job's approach to his despair, something quite different from what we see in his wife's behaviour. When we think about the actors who surround Job in this drama, his wife is quite the character. Judging by her response to the tragic series of events—*"Curse God and die"* (Job 2:9)—she seems to share Satan's view of human nature. From her vantage point, it makes perfect sense for a person to be pious and loyal to God *only* if it leads to a rich and happy life. According to this view, take away the tangible rewards of true devotion and it isn't worth it.

Job, however, demonstrates that he is willing to worship and serve God even if there are no tangible rewards. He's still all-in for God. But he wants clarification on how things are being run, because the circumstances of his life are too bizarre to grasp. He genuinely wants to know what crimes he has committed to warrant this level of punishment. A little misfortune here and there along the way, sure, but this dump trunk load of damage? Wow!

Nevertheless, as much as Job struggles to find meaning in a life rocked with pain and sorrow, some believers in the history of the Christian church have found plenty of purpose amidst their suffering.

Take Joni Eareckson Tada, for example. If you don't know her story, here it is in a nutshell. Right after her high school graduation, Joni suffered a diving accident in Chesapeake Bay. She misjudged the depth of the water and broke her neck as she dove in. The incident left her a quadriplegic. The next two years of her life were spent in therapy, rehabilitation, suicidal wishes, and anger with God.

Eventually, encouraged by friends to walk with Jesus through her trial, Joni surrendered her broken life to the Lord. Her walk of faith for more than fifty years has been extremely challenging, but the Lord has strengthened her to accomplish more in a wheelchair than most of us will ever achieve totally healthy. She's written more than forty-eight books full of wisdom and inspiration for hurting souls, recorded fifteen musical albums, launched a remarkable mouth-painting art career, started a huge ministry for the disabled community, and developed a speaking and broadcasting career. She has no less than twenty-two distinguished awards as well as numerous honorary doctoral degrees. Incredible woman!

In some ways, it may not be fair to compare Job with Joni, since Joni has so much more divine revelation than Job had. Unlike Joni, Job didn't know what Jesus was going to do on the cross. He didn't have a full picture of Christ's resurrection and victory over sin and death. Job didn't know about a believer's future hope of being given a transformed physical body in the resurrection and living eternally with God on a new earth.

Obviously, these divinely revealed truths have strengthened Joni in her spiritual journey as she has processed her sorrow and disappointment. Nevertheless, her ability to see and pursue so many purposeful avenues amidst her suffering is remarkable, especially considering the added burden of cancer over the last decade.

Still, as many incredible feats as Joni has accomplished through the power of Christ, she too has questioned God repeatedly about his sovereign love and her dire circumstances. Such a response is only natural.

It's perfectly acceptable to ask God challenging questions, even with a tinge of doubt in your voice. Think of John the Baptist. He was the Kingdom of God's first-century keynote speaker and his divine cousin's right-hand man. Then he ends up in prison on death row. And when John questions Jesus about his distasteful predicament, Jesus gives him a cryptic answer and finishes with the riddle: *"And blessed is anyone who does not take offense at Me"* (Luke 7:23, NASB). Jesus seems to be telling John that he will be blessed if he doesn't stumble or get upset over the way God is running the universe. John gets very little concrete information about why he's suffering. Shortly thereafter, his earthly life ends by the blade of an executioner.

It doesn't clear everything up, but a close examination of Jesus's riddle provides a piece of the puzzle in this mystery surrounding the topic of God's sovereignty. As I've said, we need to get more comfortable embracing the mysterious in our spiritual journey. After all, the Christian walk is one of faith, whether things are going swimmingly or disappointingly.

And speaking of disappointment, this chapter beckons us to examine Job's second big question for God as he processes the great anguish of his ordeal—namely, "God, why won't you talk to me? Why don't you answer me when I call upon you? Why do you seem the most distant when I'm in my darkest hour?" Perhaps you've heard others express these same feelings of abandonment. Maybe you've felt this way yourself on occasion.

When a person experiences profound pain, conversation helps. If you have an understanding ear by your side, the load seems that much lighter. It could be said that more than vindication, or even relief from suffering, Job just wants God to show up and talk to him: *"If only God would speak"* (Job 11:5).

You can tell by his tone that God's invisibility and silence drive Job nuts. Several times you hear him express his frustration:

I cry to you, O God, but you don't answer.
I stand before you, but you don't even look.

—Job 30:20

I go east, but he is not there.
I go west, but I cannot find him.
I do not see him in the north, for he is hidden.
I look to the south, but he is concealed.

—Job 23:8–9

In the early part of the debate, Job focuses on four themes—his innocence, his regret of having been born, his friends' lack of sympathy, and the general brevity and futility of earthly life.

But shortly into the dialogue, Job starts talking directly to God about their relationship. The tone starts off a bit snarky. One of Job's earliest depictions of God is that of a people-watcher intent on punishing wayward humans: *"If I have sinned, what have I done to you, O watcher of all humanity? Why make me your target? Am I a burden to you?"* (Job 7:20)

In a later passage, after a beautiful description of God's creative power in the womb, Job proclaims that God has ulterior motives for bringing humans into the world: *"Yet your real motive—your true intent—was to watch me, and if I sinned, you would not forgive my guilt"* (Job 10:13–14).

Fortunately, Job doesn't stay in this dark place for too long. Quite early in the text, he starts to consider what it would be like if humans could speak directly with God.

> *If someone wanted to take God to court,*
>   *would it be possible to answer him even once in a thousand times?*
>
> *For God is so wise and so mighty.*
>   *Who has ever challenged him successfully?…*
>
> *Yet when he comes near, I cannot see him.*
>   *When he moves by, I do not see him go…*
>
> *So who am I, that I should try to answer God*
>   *or even reason with him?*
> *Even if I were right, I would have no defense.*
>   *I could only plead for mercy.*

And even if I summoned him and he responded,
  I'm not sure he would listen to me.
—Job 9:3–4, 11, 14–16

But then Job has an idea:

God is not a mortal like me,
  so I cannot argue with him or take him to trial.
If only there were a mediator between us,
  someone who could bring us together.
—Job 9:32–33

However, Job's initial concept of this potential mediator is quite primitive. The best he comes up with at first is a notion of someone appearing with enough power to stop God from waling on him:

The mediator could make God stop beating me,
  and I would no longer live in terror of his punishment.
Then I could speak to him without fear,
  but I cannot do that in my own strength.
—Job 9:34–35

As much as Job laments that he cannot have a face-to-face with God, he doesn't abandon the faith he displayed in the first two chapters of the book. He keeps hounding after God for the answer rather than growing totally indifferent.

As for me, I would speak directly to the Almighty.
  I want to argue my case with God himself…
God might kill me, but I have no other hope.
  I am going to argue my case with him.
—Job 13:3, 15

Job acknowledges that he might be dead meat at the hands of the Almighty for speaking so rashly to him and demanding a chance to argue his innocence. But he claims to have no other options. There is no Plan B. Job has no hope at all apart from God. He goes on to say,

> *O God, grant me these two things,*
>   *and then I will be able to face you.*
> *Remove your heavy hand from me,*
>   *and don't terrify me with your awesome presence.*
> *Now summon me, and I will answer!*
>   *Or let me speak to you, and you reply.*
> *Tell me, what have I done wrong?*
>   *Show me my rebellion and my sin.*
> *Why do you turn away from me?*
>   *Why do you treat me as your enemy?*
>   —Job 13:20–24

At this point, Job is struggling to maintain a healthy view of God. He knows he should see the Almighty in a more amiable light, but God seems more like an enemy than a friend.

Thankfully, it doesn't take too long before this begins to change. Already by the middle of Job 16, his concept of a mediator starts to mature.

> *Even now my witness is in heaven.*
>   *My advocate is there on high.*
> *My friends scorn me,*
>   *but I pour out my tears to God.*
> *I need someone to mediate between God and me,*
>   *as a person mediates between friends.*
>   —Job 16:19–21

Lacking the fulness of New Testament theology, Job longs for what the Apostle John would eventually speak of: *"[I]f anyone does sin, we have an advocate who pleads our case before the Father. He is Jesus Christ, the one who is truly righteous"* (1 John 2:1).

Instead of a mediator who would just stop God from beating on him, Job now envisions one who might act as his witness, one who would settle the matter peacefully between the parties. Notice also that Job is hinting at the prospect of God being his friend.

The positive progression continues until it hits a high note in what has become one of the more famous passages in the book. In Job 19, we now hear him declare that he believes in the reality of a personal redeemer who can rescue him.

> *But as for me, I know that my Redeemer lives,*
> *and he will stand upon the earth at last.*
> *And after my body has decayed,*
> *yet in my body I will see God!*
> *I will see him for myself.*
> *Yes, I will see him with my own eyes.*
> *I am overwhelmed at the thought!*
> —Job 19:25–27

In ancient near east culture, a redeemer was a fixer, someone who saw something that was wrong or unfair and felt obliged to do something about it. Naturally, the word at that time didn't yet have the full New Testament meaning of a redeemer who saves sinful souls from eternal punishment, but Job's declaration at this point is lightyears ahead of where he started out.

To be fair, there are some textual challenges in this passage that render it difficult to translate. It is impossible to know exactly what Job is saying here about his redeemer. But suffice to say that Job is making significant progress in his thinking about who God is and how he is committed to Job's well-being. He went from seeing God as a cop on the beat, watching bad guys in the neighbourhood in order to bust them, to an interceding umpire who breaks up lopsided fights to a mediator who might act more like a friendly advocate. Finally, he comes to the notion of a redeemer who is fundamentally committed to justice and fairness. This redeemer, in the end, would feel obliged to take Job's side and set things right.

For Job, these proclamations lie only in the domain of wishful hopes. His physical reality is that he is still stuck in the muck, scraping the pus off his scabs, writhing in pain, reliving his nightmares of loss with no divine audible response forthcoming.

> *If only I knew where to find God,*
> *I would go to his court.*
> *I would lay out my case*
> *and present my arguments.*
> *Then I would listen to his reply*
> *and understand what he says to me.*
> *Would he use his great power to argue with me?*
> *No, he would give me a fair hearing.*
> *Honest people can reason with him,*
> *so I would be forever acquitted by my judge.*
>
> —Job 23:3–7

Even though he's frustrated that he cannot find God, near the end of the debate with his friends Job's view of Yahweh circles back to that of being a fair judge. He's starting to see the Lord in a similar fashion to how he perceived him before the great stock market crash of his life. Notice that he speaks of God as being reasonable and fair.

The only problem is that Job still cannot find him, so the trial of vindication will likely never happen.

His concluding thoughts on the matter are found in his final speech:

> *If only someone would listen to me!*
> *Look, I will sign my name to my defense.*
> *Let the Almighty answer me.*
> *Let my accuser write out the charges against me.*
> *I would face the accusation proudly.*
> *I would wear it like a crown.*
> *For I would tell him exactly what I have done.*
> *I would come before him like a prince.*
> —Job 31:35–37

To help us empathize with our sad central character, I've laid out a detailed presentation of Job's thoughts regarding God's apparent reticence amidst human trials. Being attuned to Job's deepest emotions of frustration, how might we respond to his dilemma? What is the answer to Job's questions regarding God's supposed silence? What do we tell people who wonder why they feel God has abandoned them in their darkest hour?

This is tricky. Entering this conversation with suffering souls is made complicated by the prominence of emotions in the modern-day psyche. In the philosophical development of modern Western thought, sentiment and personal experience have come to take top billing over rational absolute truth. There seems to be less and less potency in merely reassuring a wounded heart of the theological certainty of God's ever-present nature.

However, that should not stop one from trying.

One starting point might be the following general observation, which is probably best posed as a question. Did Job consider God more talkative when he was healthy and wealthy than when he was suffering? Did he *hear from God* more when things were going well?

Did God talk to him repeatedly while he sipped his Perrier with the paychecks rolling in? Or did he just assume God's presence because there were no signs of trouble? How much effort do we make to hear from God during prosperity and success? Why do we claim to feel God's presence when things are going well yet announce his abandonment when we suffer?

Secondly, we must acknowledge that Job does a lot of things right. Despite his anger, he does something many struggle to do: he rushes *to* God in his rage, not *away*.

Anger with God arouses some very common responses from the human soul. Disillusioned travellers are more likely to avoid God than to have it out with him. Bible reading and prayer go cold and victims nestle into a bed of complaints and bitterness. When people are disappointed by the downturns of life, the greatest temptation is to forget God and then self-medicate with food, pills, alcohol, Netflix, or porn.

But Job does not shut God out. Nor does he get lost in bouts of self-pity and cynicism. Instead he continues to call out to God for answers, relief, and reassurance. Forcefully, he demands that God lay his cards on the table.

Most importantly, he refuses to get out of God's face. Just as John the Baptist brought his question straight to Jesus when he was distraught, Job continues to lay his complaints before God. That is what sustains his relationship with the Almighty even when it seems that the phone line has been currently disconnected.

And though neither Job nor we perceive it, God evidently does show up and begin to bring healing. Ultimately, it's not the suffering that makes Job a better person. What makes him a better person is God's presence in the suffering. Imagine where Job would have ended up if he had totally frozen God out.

Clearly, Job doesn't do everything right, but he keeps himself pointed in the right direction—and that made all the difference. When he finally gets his appointment with God and is confronted with the Lord's undeniable and incomprehensible sovereignty, Job readily repents and humbles himself before his Maker. You see, all along, his heart was in the right place, even though it was severely broken.

Careful examination of the verbal sparring between Job and his friends yields one final and fascinating observation. Throughout the narrative, Job talks with his friends and he talks *to* God. In contrast, the friends just talk to Job *about* God. The companions know their traditional theology; Job wants to go beyond it and truly know his God.

And because Job is so committed to his relationship with Yahweh, God's grace mysteriously works in his life despite his feelings of distance from the Almighty throughout the whole ordeal. Even though Job may not have noticed it at the time, we can see it in the progression of his dialogue. Job is changing in the process. He is getting better.

So what do we say to our hurting colleagues who feel God has left them alone in their pain? Well, as few words as possible. We must allow them to express their emotions honestly without being dealt a clichéd answer.

But if you must speak, encourage those enduring great hardship to pursue God persistently with reckless abandon. Keep asking him good questions. Express emotions honestly. Humbly accept the fact that, from our vantage point, there will always be some mystery involved in the concept of God's sovereignty.

Most importantly, encourage them to keep everything pointed in the right direction—toward the Almighty, the all-wise, infinite, immutable, sovereign Lord of heaven's armies.

From our vantage point, here's something else worth pondering: even Jesus on the cross, at the exact moment of his deepest suffering, asked his Father why he had been abandoned. In that excruciating event, Jesus as a human felt the pain of suffering in the darkness. He felt alone and forsaken.

Because the Son of God remained true to his followers in his darkest moment, they can remain true to him, trusting in his abiding love even when it doesn't look or feel present. For those willing to listen, the Divine One always speaks words of comfort: "Do not abandon me, because no matter how it feels, I have not abandoned you."

QUESTIONS FOR GOD

Round Three

Studying the Book of Job tosses us into a whirlwind of opinions about the sovereignty of God, particularly how it relates to human pain and suffering. Amidst the debris of such a windy discussion, we may notice that there is a human tendency to simplify God in the story. As we talk about the Almighty, we are tempted to present him as a really good human as opposed to seeing him for who he truly is—the eternal, transcendent, all-knowing, all-powerful, ever-present Creator, Sustainer, and Judge of the universe.

Because of this human inclination to make God smaller than he is, the Book of Job seems to present us with all sorts of theological problems. When we equate God to an extremely benevolent human, we cannot imagine him getting suckered into a bet with Satan that plunges a godly man into untold suffering. To our human logic, it seems so unfair. As loving people, we try to stop preventable evil from happening to our children and those we care for. So why wouldn't God do the same?

Here's the problem with this logic: when we try to put the phrase *is like* between the words *God* and *human*, we're headed for all sorts of trouble. For God is not a super great human. He is not the best of what humans can assemble. He is God. He is the source of everything. To see God as a superior human is as silly as seeing a potter as a superior piece of clay. We've got the Maker and the thing that is made. We cannot confuse the two. They are on different levels.

The sovereignty of God isn't a super organized plan for everything to go swell for everybody on the planet, and the love of God is not just a mushy, feel-good emotional experience where warm sensations pour over us.

The sovereignty and goodness of God have meanings beyond human notions of control and compassion. Just because we think we would do something in a situation doesn't mean that God is obliged to do the same.

As clichéd as it might sound to a veteran Christian, the words of the prophet Isaiah are still true regarding the unparalleled supremacy of God's decision-making faculties:

> *"My thoughts are nothing like your thoughts," says the Lord.*
> *"And my ways are far beyond anything you could imagine.*
> *For just as the heavens are higher than the earth,*
> *so my ways are higher than your ways*
> *and my thoughts higher than your thoughts."*
> —Isaiah 55:8–9

To pretend that we understand exactly what God had in mind for Job is to do exactly that—pretend. We can speculate.

But our guesses must be framed within the truth of his divine, sovereign love. And our understanding of his sovereign love will always be shrouded in murkiness. Our willingness to live within this mystery is a barometer of our humility. To truly absorb the theology of this saga, one must humbly bow before God and submit totally to him.

If a twenty-first century observer struggles to get their head around the story of Job, imagine how difficult it was for the man himself, not knowing anything about the heavenly discussion.

His first big question, asked more than once, has become a classic in the world of theological debate: "What's the use of living when your life is so plagued with pain and suffering? Why does God allow faithful believers to suffer enormously or experience unfair tragedies?"

The answer to that question often becomes more evident with time. Though the person suffering may never see a purpose for the trial, it can become clearer.

Case in point, John the Baptist. To the average mind in first-century Judea, and probably the mind of John himself, it would have made perfect sense for him to be released from prison so he could be out there, enjoying the big Kingdom of God party with his cousin Jesus and all his followers. It must have seemed strange at the time for God to allow the rock star of the movement to be taken out of the way so quickly.

But when we look at the story from our vantage point, it makes sense for John to be removed from the scene. If he had not, there would have been all sorts of confusion and loyalty issues amidst the movement's followers. Because of John's big personality, his exclusion delivered a clear message—any wannabe disciples who desired to become part of the Kingdom of God had to follow Jesus as their one and only true leader.

Time has also given us the ability to see Job's story from a wider perspective. As dark as Job's path was for those months or years, God was working in his life, refining a precious jewel to an even greater lustre. God was also showing every human who would live after Job that it's possible to possess a godly faith that isn't connected to one's circumstances. Contrary to what the accuser of the brethren claimed, Job was willing to serve God for nothing. His example of steadfast endurance has buoyed countless suffering saints for centuries.

Beyond the angst of Job's search for meaning amidst horrendous pain, he also wrestles with God's apparent absence during his troubles. Job cries out passionately for God to show up and explain the situation.

His second big question has become the cry of so many suffering believers: "Why has God abandoned me in my trial? Why does he seem to be so distant when I need him the most?" Room must be given for those in agony to express candidly how they feel amidst their severe pain and disappointment.

As much as it may appear that the Lord is missing in action while Job labours through his dark valley, he's not without God's continual presence. We will flesh out this idea more thoroughly in a later chapter, but suffice to say that Job's evolving concept of a mediator between God and man testifies to a heart that is softening, a faith that is growing, and a mind that is becoming wiser.

Still, even as he makes spiritual progress, Job continues to face the physical anguish of his illness. In his own words, *"My body is covered with maggots and scabs. My skin breaks open, oozing with pus"* (Job 7:5).

Wallowing in his sorrow, Job is compelled to ask God his third big question: "Why do the wicked so often prosper? Considering how terrible things are going for me right now, why do the bad guys around me get to have a life of ease? Why are they rewarded favourably for committing so much naughtiness? God, they are ignoring and even despising you! What is the point of being righteous if there is no guarantee of a nice life in return?"

In almost every speech made by Job's friends, these self-assured sages remind him of the accepted theology of the day—namely, "God is committed to wiping out bad guys while making sure things go well for the good guys." In his very first speech, Eliphaz says what all three friends arrogantly repeat:

> *Stop and think! Do the innocent die?*
>   *When have the upright been destroyed?*
> *My experience shows that those who plant trouble*
>   *and cultivate evil will harvest the same.*

> *A breath from God destroys them.*
> *They vanish in a blast of his anger.*
>
> —Job 4:7–9

Further on in the debate, Eliphaz adds:

> *The wicked writhe in pain throughout their lives.*
> *Years of trouble are stored up for the ruthless…*
>
> *They will be cut down in the prime of life;*
> *their branches will never again be green.*
>
> —Job 15:20, 32

The friends imply that their pristine theology proves Job is guilty of something, and it's his duty now to confess his sin. If he does, God will bring back the sunny skies of his good old days.

In the face of this repeated barrage of criticism, Job eventually snaps. He can't take it anymore. He wants his friends to wake up to the fact that lots of bad guys never receive their judgment in this life.

> *Why do the wicked prosper,*
> *growing old and powerful?*
> *They live to see their children grow up and settle down,*
> *and they enjoy their grandchildren.*
> *Their homes are safe from every fear,*
> *and God does not punish them.*
> *Their bulls never fail to breed.*
> *Their cows bear calves and never miscarry.*
> *They let their children frisk about like lambs.*
> *Their little ones skip and dance.*
> *They sing with tambourine and harp.*
> *They celebrate to the sound of the flute.*

> They spend their days in prosperity,
>> then go down to the grave in peace.
>
> —Job 21:7–13

Adding insult to injury, Job is annoyed by the fact that while these rich wicked men are becoming wicked rich, they routinely tell God to take a hike.

> And yet they say to God, "Go away.
>> We want no part of you and your ways.
> Who is the Almighty, and why should we obey him?
>> What good will it do us to pray?"
> (They think their prosperity is of their own doing,
>> but I will have nothing to do with that kind of thinking.)
>
> Yet the light of the wicked never seems to be extinguished.
>> Do they ever have trouble?
>> Does God distribute sorrows to them in anger?
> Are they driven before the wind like straw?
>> Are they carried away by the storm like chaff?
>> Not at all!
>
> —Job 21:14–18

In the back and forth bickering between Job and his friends regarding the matter, both parties claim to have history, personal observation, and common sense on their side. But Job says, "Look, fellas, I know there may be a few rich guys out there who have suffered an early or untimely demise, but most evil people who are rich enjoy a pretty good life."

> Look, I know what you're thinking.
>> I know the schemes you plot against me.

> *You will tell me of rich and wicked people*
> > *whose houses have vanished because of their sins.*
> *But ask those who have been around,*
> > *and they will tell you the truth.*
> *Evil people are spared in times of calamity*
> > *and are allowed to escape disaster.*
> *No one criticizes them openly*
> > *or pays them back for what they have done.*
> *When they are carried to the grave,*
> > *an honor guard keeps watch at their tomb.*
> *A great funeral procession goes to the cemetery.*
> > *Many pay their respects as the body is laid to rest,*
> *and the earth gives sweet repose.*
> > > —Job 21:27–33

Job laments that even in death the wealthy wicked are honoured and remembered well.

At this point, he might be thinking about what the end of his own life is going to look like. The way things are going, he can't envision a happy ending to his story. At one low point, he lists the forces that are working against him—his friends mock and accuse him, his relatives stay away, his servants and maids will no longer answer his call, his wife can't stand his breath, and even little children have learned to despise him (Job 19:13–19). He feels that everyone he's ever loved has turned against him. He can't imagine his funeral being anything but a gong show.

Have you ever felt this way, wondering why righteous behaviour can sometimes end in material disaster while sinful practices produce a financially prosperous outcome? We want to believe that God will bless virtuous behaviour. It makes sense to a rational brain. We may not tell anyone that we expect God to pay a financial return for our uprightness, but certainly it feels strange to have good deeds rewarded with economic failure. Why is it so common to hear of crooked people in business who ruthlessly respond to the kindness and generosity of their partners with travesty and betrayal, taking all the money and running?

My wife and I are friends with a couple who live on Vancouver Island and own a printing business. They're very good Christian people who always treat their employees with decency and fairness. Yet their first business was lost to a struggle with greedy employees who wanted to unionize the staff and strip the company bare. Our friends lost everything, years of monetary and sweat equity. After more than a decade, they had to start over from scratch. It was a sad illustration of the wicked getting away with their wickedness and the righteous suffering unfairly.

It was a very challenging time for our friends. As patient and morally upright as they remained throughout the ordeal, they couldn't help but wonder why God often delays the defence of the righteous and the judgment of the wicked. Job had similar thoughts as he reflected on what evil people will do to attain their wealth.

> *Why doesn't the Almighty bring the wicked to judgment?*
> > *Why must the godly wait for him in vain?*
> *Evil people steal land by moving the boundary markers.*
> > *They steal livestock and put them in their own pastures.*
> *They take the orphan's donkey*
> > *and demand the widow's ox as security for a loan.*
> *The poor are pushed off the path;*
> > *the needy must hide together for safety...*
>
> *The wicked snatch a widow's child from her breast,*
> > *taking the baby as security for a loan.*

The poor must go about naked, without any clothing.
   They harvest food for others while they themselves are starving.
They press out olive oil without being allowed to taste it,
   and they tread in the winepress as they suffer from thirst.
The groans of the dying rise from the city,
   and the wounded cry for help,
yet God ignores their moaning.
—Job 24:1–4, 9–12

Much of the Old Testament talks about the special place God has in his heart for the needy and oppressed. Even though Job wasn't able to read those Scriptures, since they most likely weren't written yet, he had an innate sense of justice about how things should be. And yet, the righteous poor are often victimized by the criminally wicked wealthy.

From a New Testament perspective, rich in theological truth about the afterlife and the final judgment of God's enemies, Christian believers should be able to handle the riddle of wicked prosperity with greater ease than Job could. Yet he still had hope that God would eventually take care of business.

As if starting to regain his faith, Job concludes his argument with these words of hope:

God, in his power, drags away the rich.
   They may rise high, but they have no assurance of life.
They may be allowed to live in security,
   but God is always watching them.
And though they are great now,
   in a moment they will be gone like all others,
cut off like heads of grain.
—Job 24:22–24

When we're healthy and doing relatively well, it's hard enough to process the injustice of the wicked prospering. Imagine the difficulty of doing so amidst what Job endured. How can we believe God is just, sovereign, and loving when he runs a world where nasty people get away with so much? Why does the Almighty allow criminals to amass illicit fortunes? Must we simply accept this staggering reality or are we entitled to a better explanation of God's sovereignty?

As I have already asked, what do we truly deserve in this life? Do we deserve for things to go well for us as long as we behave as good little Christians? Do we deserve an answer from God about this particularly perplexing matter? Should the Lord rise up and clarify for us exactly what's going on in his rule of the universe?

In his book on Job, subtitled *When Bad Things Happened to a Good Person*, Harold S. Kushner writes,

> If we by our righteous behaviour, could compel God to treat us well, to bless us with health and prosperity and guard our children from harm, would he still be the all-powerful Master of the Universe? Or would he be reduced to some supercomputer capable of doing awesome things beyond the capacity of any human being, but only if we tell it to? Would we have turned God into a cosmic vending machine: insert the proper number of good deeds—prayer, charity, forgiveness of those who hurt us—pull the plunger for the blessing you want, and if you don't get it, feel entitled to curse the machine and take your business elsewhere?[11]

I think Kushner is spot on here. God can't be reduced to some form of cosmic vending machine. Simple logic tells us that such a

---

[11] Harold S. Kushner, *The Book of Job* (New York, NY: Schocken Books, 2012), 69.

system of divine sovereignty could never operate like this. It's totally unworkable.

Imagine two Christian high school basketball teams playing against each other in a provincial or state championship game. Both teams have paid their moral dues, so to speak. Equally, they have displayed good attitudes throughout the season and maintained an excellent work ethic during practice times. They have faithfully respected their coaches and performed unselfish acts of service in their communities. Both have even committed their entire season to the glory of God.

Now, who is God going to reward with the victory?

Humans do not, and will never in this life, have a full handle on how God runs the show. There is no predictable and repeatable formula. For many reasons, this subject will always involve some mystery. There does seem to be some chance involved; for example, a baseball hitting an irregular spot in the turf can win or lose the World Series. Also, God has clearly equipped humans with free will to choose good or evil. And sometimes a semitruck will hit a bus full of young hockey players.

Once again, people of Christian faith today have the upper hand on Job. The full measure of Scripture now available reveals that life is not a simple thing to figure out. It's complex, with intricacies rooted in two factors always at play in the affairs of the world.

First, everything in life has been created by God. So yes, there is order in the world. If you work hard, your faithful labour will often be rewarded with proportionate wealth. If you plant your crops and water them well, you will often reap a decent harvest. If you treat people kindly, you will often enjoy good relationships. If Christians raise their children to fear and honour the Lord, often they will stay true to him as they get older.

But that is only one rail on the track. One truth.

The other rail revealed in God's Word is less delightful: everything in the world is fallen. The current system is broken in so many ways, and there is evil present everywhere. Sometimes you work hard and are not rewarded. The backstabbing, snively suck-up from across the office may get the promotion you deserved. Sometimes you sacrificially pour your life into being a wonderful, supportive partner and your spouse leaves you anyway. Sometimes Christians exert enormous effort to raise their kids to follow Jesus and the little monkeys walk away from the whole scene. Sometimes you do everything right and everything goes wrong.

There is evil in the world. And there is order.

Life is a train that rides both these rails, so one's own personal narrative must be lived somewhere within the messiness of both these truths, experiencing the implications of both rails. And the wise person possesses a competency regarding this complex nature of human existence.

It feels like cheating to say that the answer to a paradoxical question is another paradox. To the human brain, which craves rationality, such an explanation is less than fulfilling. But maybe that's the point. Maybe that's the true essence of Christian faith—abandoning the security of our either/or systems in logic and embracing the paradoxical nature of divine truth. If faith made perfect sense to the rational mind, it wouldn't be called faith.

Perhaps the simplest definition of Christian faith is to call it the act of trusting God implicitly while facing the confusions of life, trusting God that, amidst this ordered and disordered world, his sovereignty is inevitably bathed in his love for us. Is that a tall order? Maybe. But as Job knows only too well, and as the Bible explains in numerous places, the hard way may be the right way.

So as we continue to live within this mystery and, along with Job, watch many wicked people live lives of unencumbered prosperity, there may be some value in hearing the testimony of another biblical writer who wrestled fiercely with this topic and came out on top. Listen to words of the psalmist Asaph. The passage is long but worth the ride.

> *But as for me, I almost lost my footing.*
>   *My feet were slipping, and I was almost gone.*
> *For I envied the proud*
>   *when I saw them prosper despite their wickedness.*
> *They seem to live such painless lives;*
>   *their bodies are so healthy and strong.*
> *They don't have troubles like other people;*
>   *they're not plagued with problems like everyone else.*
> *They wear pride like a jeweled necklace*
>   *and clothe themselves with cruelty.*
> *These fat cats have everything*
>   *their hearts could ever wish for!*
> *They scoff and speak only evil;*
>   *in their pride they seek to crush others.*
> *They boast against the very heavens,*
>   *and their words strut throughout the earth.*
> *And so the people are dismayed and confused…*
>
> *"What does God know?" they ask.*
>   *"Does the Most High even know what's happening?"*
> *Look at these wicked people—*
>   *enjoying a life of ease while their riches multiply.*
> *Did I keep my heart pure for nothing?*
>   *Did I keep myself innocent for no reason?*
> *I get nothing but trouble all day long;*
>   *every morning brings me pain.*

If I had really spoken this way to others,
*   I would have been a traitor to your people.*
So I tried to understand why the wicked prosper.
*   But what a difficult task it is!*
Then I went into your sanctuary, O God,
*   and I finally understood the destiny of the wicked.*
Truly, you put them on a slippery path
*   and send them sliding over the cliff to destruction.*
In an instant they are destroyed,
*   completely swept away by terrors.*
When you arise, O Lord,
*   you will laugh at their silly ideas*
*   as a person laughs at dreams in the morning.*

Then I realized that my heart was bitter,
*   and I was all torn up inside.*
I was so foolish and ignorant—
*   I must have seemed like a senseless animal to you.*
Yet I still belong to you;
*   you hold my right hand.*
You guide me with your counsel,
*   leading me to a glorious destiny.*
Whom have I in heaven but you?
*   I desire you more than anything on earth.*
My health may fail, and my spirit may grow weak,
*   but God remains the strength of my heart;*
*   he is mine forever…*

I have made the Sovereign Lord my shelter…
    —Psalm 73:2–26, 28

Asaph learned how to settle his heart on this matter. When he was tempted to languish over the injustice of the wicked being allowed to prosper, he went into God's presence and found comfort in what he knew to be true.

Sure, you're going to witness many proud, scoffing, evil people live comfy lives of ease. But don't get worked up over it. It won't always be this way. A day of reckoning will come, and it will be terrible.

On the flip side, those who walk closely with God have the unique pleasure of becoming his possession; he holds their hand and guides their way.

And the punchline? You can't go wrong when you desire God more than anything on earth, especially riches. Even when health and wealth fail, hearts are made strong by being in his presence. Therefore, we come to Asaph's thesis: make the sovereign Lord your shelter.

As messy as the Book of Job can look at times, he does exactly what Asaph declared years later in his beautiful psalm. Amidst the chaos of his life, Job makes the sovereign Lord his shelter. He keeps bringing his troubles and concerns to the Father. He never leaves God's presence or takes the Almighty out of the equation.

And though Job never gets answers to any of his questions, in the end, when he meets God in all his greatness and glory, the unanswered questions no longer matter. All that matters is God himself, the eternal shelter.

WITH FRIENDS LIKE THESE...

Studying the Book of Job is a challenging adventure for both rookie and veteran theologian alike. It's not uncommon to feel uncomfortable with the degree of suffering Job experiences. Even if you think you have a strong stomach for God's sovereignty, it's hard to swallow the reality of Job's torment. Our gag reflexes go into motion as we try to come to terms with why God allowed Satan to ramp up the craziness to this level.

As westerners, susceptible to a prosperity gospel, we prefer God to be more of a generous, galactic, good-times dispenser than a sovereign Ruler of the universe. We mistakenly compare God's reign over all creation to our reign over the affairs in our little domains.

Using our own motives and tactics as performance appraisal tools, we proceed to measure God's competency according to the quality of our circumstances. Often, we give him a bad review. We're puzzled when things don't turn out as we think they should.

To put it bluntly, we cannot stomach God acting in a way we think we would not.

Despite our struggle to understand God's loving sovereignty amidst human suffering, modern-day Christians are privileged to view Job's challenges through a broader lens. From Matthew, we understand that God *"gives his sunlight to both the evil and the good, and he sends rain on the just and the unjust alike"* (Matthew 5:45).

From the bulk of New Testament teaching, believers now cling to the hope of an eternal blessed future with Jesus and lay claim to the indwelling Holy Spirit who ministers comfort and wisdom in times of trouble. Moreover, any well-versed theologian today understands that there is both order and disorder in our wonderfully created yet sadly fallen world.

All these truths are now part of the spiritual psyche of Christendom. It's like contemporary Christians are flying first class in a fully crewed Boeing 747 while Job flew solo in his little Cessna 180.

Without the theological richness of thousands of years of divine revelation, Job's experience was focused on simple faith in God. Accordingly, Job expressed himself honestly before the Lord with heated emotion. The fact that God allowed him to spew his tirade for dozens of chapters teaches us something about God's ability to tolerate our tough questions.

There is great merit in letting hurting people pour out their aching soul without the emotional restrictions of pat answers. Allowing suffering people to ask the right questions can often bring more healing to the hurting soul than hearing the right answers.

The importance of listening to the cries of hurting souls is at the heart of this ancient dialogue, and Job's friends totally fail in this area. Consequently, Job ends up bearing the brunt of having comforters who sound more like enemies than friends.

But it doesn't start that way. When they first arrive on the scene, we are sympathetic to the friends and their initial respect for Job and his deep level of suffering.

> When three of Job's friends heard of the tragedy he had suffered, they got together and traveled from their homes to comfort and console him. Their names were Eliphaz the Temanite, Bildad the Shuhite, and Zophar the Naamathite. When they saw Job from a distance, they scarcely recognized him. Wailing

loudly, they tore their robes and threw dust into the air over their heads to show their grief. Then they sat on the ground with him for seven days and nights. No one said a word to Job, for they saw that his suffering was too great for words.

—Job 2:11–13

At first, the friends care enough to organize a plan to get themselves to Job's house. They cry vociferously. They rip their clothes and throw dirt on their heads as part of the culturally approved mourning ritual. For seven days, they are sensitive enough to keep their mouths shut. There is a powerful and comforting witness in silent presence, and the friends do it well.

For a spell.

To be fair, it doesn't appear that the friends deliberately intend to pick a fight with Job. As the text affirms, they want *"to comfort and console him"* (Job 2:11). They want to help him feel better. They hope he receives a complete reversal of fortune. They expect that Job will find their words soothing, and that their advice will help alleviate his anguish.

But once the dialogue gets going, their initial sympathetic intentions trickle away. They gradually harden their hearts and get stuck in a rut of their own making. Refusing to veer from their prejudice, they stubbornly profess that only two of the following three statements can ever be true at the same time:

1. God is all-powerful.
2. God is completely good.
3. Suffering exists in the life of a righteous person.

All four men agree with the first point. While Job struggles with the second, God's goodness, the friends target the third and challenge Job's righteousness.

At the outset, Job acknowledges that his suffering comes from the hand of God. He simply wants the Lord, or someone else, to make sense of the punishment, to tell him what he has done to deserve such misery. Once he knows, he'll be happy to repent. Job doesn't want to believe that God makes mistakes, or even that good people might suffer for no apparent reason. Considering himself to be innocent, he is confused.

The friends stick to their story, never wavering from what they believe to be true—namely, a good God never allows a morally upright person to suffer to the extent Job suffers. Because such harsh punishment is only intended for the wicked, they conclude that Job must be concealing wickedness in his life. The friends' formula is neat and tidy. They have no interest in adjusting their thinking based on what Job tells them. Their theology is fixed, having learned it from their elders and their own experience.

Eliphaz, likely the oldest, is the first to speak. Initially, he advises Job to man up and take some of his own medicine, so to speak.

> *In the past you have encouraged many people;*
> * you have strengthened those who were weak.*
> *Your words have supported those who were falling;*
> * you encouraged those with shaky knees.*
> *But now when trouble strikes, you lose heart.*
> * You are terrified when it touches you.*
>
> —Job 4:3–5

Eliphaz wants Job to heed the same advice he has given others in the past. When disaster strikes, it's time to self-examine, because God may be addressing some sin in your life.

In addition to this exhortation, Eliphaz endeavours to boost Job's spirits by assuring him that his overall integrity should give him confidence about the future.

Doesn't your reverence for God give you confidence?
    Doesn't your life of integrity give you hope?

Stop and think! Do the innocent die?
    When have the upright been destroyed?

—Job 4:6–7

Basically, he says, "Job, you're a pretty good guy. If you just repent, everything will turn out fine."

Eliphaz goes on to explain that because God judges his angels who sin, he will certainly judge mere mortals when they sin (Job 4:18–19). He even adds a comment that we typically associate with the writer of the Book of Hebrews in the New Testament: *"But consider the joy of those corrected by God! Do not despise the discipline of the Almighty when you sin"* (Job 5:17).

The theology of the friends has no alternate interpretation for the observed situation at hand. Right from the start, they assume Job's guilt. This posture surprises Job, for he anticipated their unwavering support. Besides abruptly declaring *"Stop assuming my guilt"* (Job 6:29), Job proceeds to spell out how friends are supposed to behave in these tough situations.

One should be kind to a fainting friend,
    but you accuse me without any fear of the Almighty.
My brothers, you have proved as unreliable as a seasonal brook
    that overflows its banks in the spring
when it is swollen with ice and melting snow.
But when the hot weather arrives, the water disappears.
    The brook vanishes in the heat.
The caravans turn aside to be refreshed…

> *They count on it but are disappointed.*
> > *When they arrive, their hopes are dashed.*
> *You, too, have given no help.*
> > —Job 6:14–18, 20–21

Job is disappointed in the barrenness of his friends' words. His hopes have been dashed. He counted on their relief, but they prove themselves unreliable. Yes, Job is wearing his big-boy tunic. He's mature enough to handle the truth. He can even cope with their candid approach, but he wants proof of his misconduct.

> *Teach me, and I will keep quiet.*
> > *Show me what I have done wrong.*
> *Honest words can be painful,*
> > *but what do your criticisms amount to?*
> *Do you think your words are convincing*
> > *when you disregard my cry of desperation?*
> > —Job 6:24–26

Completely ignoring everything Job has just said, the next friend begins his oration with a cutting remark. Bildad rudely asks, *"How long will you go on like this? You sound like a blustering wind"* (Job 8:2). Adding insult to injury, he throws in a cruel comment about Job's kids: *"Your children must have sinned against him, so their punishment was well deserved"* (Job 8:4). It's hard to imagine someone having less compassion and sensitivity to a friend's plight. You lose all your children and then your friend says your kids deserved to die? Unbelievable.

And Zophar doesn't do any better. In his first speech, he adds nothing new to the conversation except a personal dig at Job, telling him that, considering how wicked he must be, he's getting off easy: *"God is doubtless punishing you far less than you deserve!"* (Job 11:6)

But the good news, says Zophar, is that Job can free himself of his suffering if he just repents:

> *If only you would prepare your heart*
> *　　and lift up your hands to him in prayer!*
> *Get rid of your sins,*
> *　　and leave all iniquity behind you.*
> *Then your face will brighten with innocence.*
> *　　You will be strong and free of fear.*
> *You will forget your misery;*
> *　　it will be like water flowing away.*
> *Your life will be brighter than the noonday.*
> *　　Even darkness will be as bright as morning.*
> 　　　　　　　　　　　　—Job 11:13–17

Job begins his response to Zophar with a zinger of his own:

> *You people really know everything, don't you?*
> *　　And when you die, wisdom will die with you!*
> *Well, I know a few things myself—*
> *　　and you're no better than I am.*
> *　　Who doesn't know these things you've been saying?*
> *Yet my friends laugh at me,*
> *　　for I call on God and expect an answer.*
> *I am a just and blameless man,*
> *　　yet they laugh at me.*
> *People who are at ease mock those in trouble.*
> *　　They give a push to people who are stumbling.*
> 　　　　　　　　　　　　—Job 12:2–5

It's easy to have all the answers when things are going well for you. Pleasant circumstances can deceptively empower onlookers to be critical and judgmental. Job's friends are confident they have a handle on the good life, so they repeatedly spew forth harsh words to get Job to crack and confess his crimes. Because they bring nothing but grief to his already sorrowful state, Job can only say, *"As for you, you smear me with lies. As physicians, you are worthless quacks. If only you could be silent! That's the wisest thing you could do"* (Job 13:4–5).

Continuing with his unfavorable assessment of the friends' speeches, Job proceeds to say perhaps some of the most intriguing and wisest words in the entire book:

> *Are you defending God with lies?*
> > *Do you make your dishonest arguments for his sake?*
> *Will you slant your testimony in his favor?*
> > *Will you argue God's case for him?*
> *What will happen when he finds out what you are doing?*
> > *Can you fool him as easily as you fool people?*
> *No, you will be in trouble with him*
> > *if you secretly slant your testimony in his favor.*
> > > —Job 13:7–10

This is the crux of the matter for these friends. They are truly defending God with lies, saying things that aren't true to fight for Yahweh's reputation. We know they aren't speaking rightly about God because the Lord says so at the end of the book.

Frankly, these friends can't handle a God who might be different from their established perception of him. They're unwilling to embrace the mystery of a good God who allows a righteous person to suffer. Refusing to submit entirely to the sovereignty of God, they remain steadfast in their portrayal of a deity who only behaves like they want him to behave.

Consequently, we will limit our exposure to the friends' comments. They get repetitive and, over time, even more nasty.

For instance, in his second speech, Bildad takes another jab at Job by calling his lack of descendants a characteristic of wickedness: *"They will have neither children nor grandchildren, nor any survivor in the place where they lived"* (Job 18:19). This sucker punch was especially cruel, considering Job's state of bereavement.

Eliphaz does no better. In his last go at Job, he refuses to entertain the possibility of Job's innocence, and in effect tells him that he is even worse morally than they originally thought. Is Job suffering unjustly? Eliphaz says, *"No, it's because of your wickedness! There's no limit to your sins"* (Job 22:5).

He then proceeds to catalogue Job's supposed crimes against all the needy and oppressed in society (Job 22:6–11). The list is a fiasco of falsehood. In response to all these goofy claims, Job can only say, *"I am surrounded by mockers. I watch how bitterly they taunt me"* (Job 17:2).

Summing up the value of the friends' deficient contribution to the dialogue, Job concludes, *"How can your empty clichés comfort me? All your explanations are lies!"* (Job 21:34) The suffering saint cries out to God as his only hope: *"You must defend my innocence, O God, since no one else will stand up for me"* (Job 17:3). This is a powerful declaration of faith in a divine being Job has never seen. Being rejected by the hurtful friends visible before him, Job embraces the invisible Almighty as his only hope of defence.

But as majestic and spiritual as this assertion may sound, the human side of Job just wants a little human help, some tangible TLC. His heart's cry is for someone to come to his side and advocate for him. He needs a buddy to step up and truly listen and empathize. He feels so alone. Desperately he cries out, *"Have mercy on me, my friends, have mercy, for the hand of God has struck me. Must you also persecute me, like God does? Haven't you chewed me up enough?"* (Job 19:21–22)

Ultimately, the friends drop the ball. After their initial seven days of silence, they provide nothing by way of comfort and encouragement. Job assures his companions that, if their roles were reversed, he would try to alleviate their grief. That is what friends do, right? They bestow mercy and compassion on those they care for.

Certainly, the friends do say many things that are true. Sections of their remarks could fit comfortably into the rhyme and timbre of any psalm. They speak eloquently about God's power, wisdom, sovereignty, and holiness. But because they mix up these theological truths with their skewed and narrow view of the relationship between God and human suffering, there ends up being a great disparity between their theology and Job's experience.

Yes, sometimes God punishes people for their rebellion, but not always. Yes, sometimes the nature of wicked conduct or bad company generates its own punishment through the natural consequences of evil. And yes, sometimes God tangibly blesses his children for their faithful witness and upright behaviour. Integrity and virtue often produce their own reward, especially in the business world. But God doesn't guarantee these things in this life.

Because of their incomplete theology, the friends fail on several levels. To begin with, we notice that Job talks both to his friends and he talks to God. The friends, however, just talk to Job *about* God. The notable difference between these characters leads us to wonder if this is the real fundamental issue at hand—Job has a relationship with God; his friends have a 4.0 GPA from their local seminary. The trio demonstrate very little of what would indicate a genuine connection with their Maker. What else could explain their deficiency of compassion and stubborn refusal to listen sincerely? They lack God's empathy for the oppressed as well as the common-sense duty to intercede for someone they supposedly love. Not once do they pray for him. They're consumed with speaking to Job on God's behalf but never once try to speak to God on Job's behalf.

Blatant in the text is the friends' repeated refusal to listen to anything Job says. And because they are ignorant of his true experience, they have nothing useful to say. Note to self: don't offer counsel when you don't understand what people are going through. Otherwise you'll just end up throwing gasoline on the fire, escalating painful feelings by saying silly things.

The relational failure of Job's friends offers an instructional seminar on how to do counselling wrong. People who see themselves as counsellors usually enter painful situations with the intent to help. But the pattern and spirit of the friends' therapeutic procedure is anything but helpful. It's a total disaster in at least three ways.

First, a person's proffered help fails when they're unwilling to let experience expand and clean up theology. The friends' God was too small. Their deity was one who simply thought exactly as they thought. They were determined to press Job's experience into the mould of their theology. Job, on the other hand, was willing to allow his experience to speak to his theological understanding.

Please hear me properly on this matter: I'm not suggesting that we are free to make up theology based solely on our own personal experience and rational deduction. I'm not talking about making truth relative to our experience. But sometimes, because of age, ignorance, or exposure to wrong teaching, our theology is incomplete and in need of enhancement.

How does that improvement happen? Most commonly, our theological deficiencies are corrected through exposure to sound teaching. Such teaching may occur informally via conversations with trusted spiritual mentors, or it may come about formally through teaching at a local church or Christian college.

And on occasion, our theological prowess can be improved through careful reflection on our own life experience. What we encounter in our journey also gives us a truer picture of who God is.

The greatest source of Job's angst is that his old well-polished theological understanding of worldly blessing crumbles beneath his feet. As he learns, the problem is not with God, but with the faulty foundation upon which he had placed God for most of his life. God's goodness and grace are not inextricably connected to good health, fat balance sheets, and peaceful family gatherings.

God's Word is inspired and authoritative, but humans aren't impeccable interpreters of it. Aspiring scholars need humility in understanding some of the more mysterious matters of God's unseen work. Presuming to know the exact mind of God leads to careless theology, especially in matters of deep human suffering.

Secondly, a person's help fails when it expresses the right words in the wrong spirit. Pastoral care can be dangerous apart from the grace and wisdom of God. The friends do manage to make many true statements. For example, Zophar presents an eloquent declaration of God's transcendence (Job 11:7–12). Yet for all its beauty, it's offered as part of a harsh attack on Job's attitude.

Because of their insensitivity, I would venture to guess that Job is more distressed by the judgmental attitude of the friends than by the actual words they speak. And because the friends have never sat where Job is sitting, their musings sound like answers that they looked up in the back of the textbook.

Besides the superficial flavour of their admonitions, there is far too much self-righteousness in the friends' analysis of Job's predicament. Job cannot find any comfort in the words of these smug advisors who elevate themselves while tearing down the one they allegedly came to help.

And thirdly, help fails when it offers only pessimism instead of hope. Job needs no assistance to move him towards despondency. He already feels that the course of life is out of his hands. Because pain speaks more candidly than peace, he pours out many emotional words as he flounders for some meaning to his situation. His friends, exasperated with his protests, say in effect, "This is God's will. You deserve it."

Is this the best they can do? Can they not find even a few sparks of hope to try to lift Job's spirits? Why can't they make a decent effort to cheer him up? Why do they seem so intent on tearing down a man they call a friend?

Their commitment to fatalism over hope is rooted in their arrogant attachment to a limited view of God's work in the world. Because their theology of God's sovereignty is entirely prescriptive, they maintain a one-track mind. For them, there's no hope for Job because he stubbornly refuses to repent. To protect their view of God's sovereignty, they crush his spirit.

Clearly, this is not the point of counsel, to flatten and belittle. The goal of counselling is to stand with someone, listen, show compassion and empathy, and offer hope. As the Apostle Paul writes in Romans 12:15, we are to *"weep with those who weep."* Or, as he says to the Galatians, we are to *"bear one another's burdens, and thereby fulfill the law of Christ"* (Galatians 6:2, NASB).

Any time someone assumes the role of a counsellor, seeking to help a hurting fellow traveller, they must be prepared to offer an attentive and empathetic ear. This unselfish, sacrificial posture is often far more valuable than a preoccupation with doctrinal theories. There may be a lot of information in a person's head that is in fact true and necessary for the situation to move in a healthy direction, but hurting souls will struggle to profit from it if it's delivered by a messenger who lacks compassion, love, and mercy.

Like Job's plea that comes from a broken heart, *"Have mercy on me, my friends, have mercy…"* (Job 19:21)

A TALE OF TWO PATHS

Studying the Book of Job causes us to wonder how we would have held up under the duress experienced by this godly man. Job's initial responses to the multifaceted tragedies are amazing. His faith never skips a beat.

With extended time in the trenches, however, comes great weight upon his soul.

Notice the concentric circles of attack Job endures. First, his possessions are picked off, one by one. While the messengers relay the bad news, perhaps Job is thinking, *That sucks! But I'm a good businessman. I can rebuild.* Then his children are wiped out by a devastating windstorm. This gut punch is immeasurably more severe than the loss of his flocks. But perhaps he's thinking amidst the grief, *Well, I'm still young enough to start over. And at least I have my health.* Nope! That's gone too. And so is a meaningful relationship with his wife. She has already cashed in and, according to Job, spouts only foolish advice.

The assault closes in on him, and then the final and supreme attack begins: the assault on his mind. In this pit of despair, Job has only two possessions: pain and time. Nothing to do but ache and think. And as he thinks, trying to make sense of the calamity, he has to deal with both the fleshly impulses of his own sinful nature and, I think it's fair to assume, spiritual warfare. Demonic influences no doubt attempt to infiltrate his fragile psyche.

Add to that the shallow theology and limited compassion of his friends, and Job finds himself in a dreadful spot.

Will we ever know why godly people suffer? It's becoming obvious that simple and straightforward answers won't be forthcoming. Also apparent are the harmful effects of holding to an incomplete theology, lazily applied with no thought for the victim's viewpoint.

Surprisingly, this book challenges the notion that God guarantees his followers health, wealth, children, and long life. In fact, we are confronted with the uncomfortable reality that our immediate temporal happiness may not be God's primary purpose. Some people find this unsettling.

Another puzzling enigma which will require some deciphering is the nature of the verdicts delivered by God at the end of the story. How are we to understand God's decision on who spoke rightly about him? Job says many harsh things about God yet receives the gold medal, while the friends say nice things about God and get the silver. And for their second-place finish, they are commanded to repent of their improper speech.

What else do we see in this ancient tale? Having read the book numerous times, I was quite surprised to only recently realize that it presents two distinct spiritual paths. These diverse paths may not be obvious to the casual reader, but they become evident with a little attentiveness. Job's path tracks upward, while his friends' path tracks downward.

At the risk of tipping my hand too early, I believe the direction of these paths is largely determined by the quality of the relationship with God held by each character in the story.

It is worth repeating that the friends speak to Job *about* God but never speak directly *to* God. Job, on the other hand, speaks both to his friends and repeatedly to God himself. The friends treat Job's suffering like a seminary case study while Job lives out the story in the presence of God. And throughout the whole trial, Job never abandons God as his only hope. Because of this faith, as chaotic as it sounds at times, God works in Job's life, bringing him gradually to a better place by the end of the story.

Let's take a closer look at these two paths. We'll start first with the trajectory of the friends, then move on to examine how Job's path took a different course.

In a nutshell, the friends start off in a good place. Their initial response was proper and decent—they show up and they shut up, sitting there silently for seven days in empathetic grief out of respect for their suffering friend. They seem to understand the power of quiet presence amidst great sorrow.

But once given the opportunity to speak, they take full advantage of it.

In the first bits of their dialogue, their tone is mildly gracious. You may recall that Eliphaz politely encourages Job to heed the same advice he has given others in the past. As a well-respected member of his community, Job had counselled many others in distress. So it is now time, says Eliphaz, for Job to partake of his own medicine. Eliphaz compliments Job on his integrity and reverence for God, but then shares a vision declaring the weakness of humans, a subtle nudge regarding Job's probable guilt in some area of his life. In the end, he encourages Job to bring up the matter before God with the hope that things will work out: *"If I were you, I would go to God and present my case to him"* (Job 5:8).

He even adds the rich theological nugget that God's disciplinary correction can be a joyful experience (Job 5:17–19) because one who walks rightly with God is inevitably protected from seven types of evil disaster—famine, war, slander, wild animals, theft, barrenness, and premature death (Job 5:19–26). While we might debate his last claim, obviously Eliphaz began the dialogue with a gentle tenor.

When Bildad gets his first chance to talk, he too tries to keep it civil. His comment about Job's children having sinned (Job 8:4) sounds harsh, but he makes the statement in light of the fact that God doesn't twist justice (Job 8:3).

Besides, knowing that Job made regular sacrifices for his children might have prompted Bildad to assume that even Job was concerned about his children's integrity. Like Eliphaz, Bildad tries to comfort Job with the fact that God forgives sinners who repent with pure hearts. He envisions Job's life getting back on track as soon as Job starts to act with full integrity (Job 8:5–6).

When Zophar joins in, the dialogue becomes a tad testier. He is less gracious than the others, calling Job a big blabbermouth in the first lines of his speech (Job 11:2–3). In Zophar's defence, he claims to be concerned for Job, afraid that his suffering friend is guilty of mocking God by claiming to be innocent. He then delivers a beautiful oration on the supreme wisdom and mystery of God (Job 11:7–12), followed by another call for Job's repentance (Job 11:13–20). If he comes clean, says Zophar, Job's confession of sin will result in a return to the good life: *"Your life will be brighter than the noonday"* (Job 11:17).

However, when the second round of speeches starts, there is a marked deterioration in the friends' civility. No longer polite, they bluntly insult Job because he won't budge from his claim of innocence. To paraphrase the content of Job 15, Eliphaz says, "You're not a very wise dude after all, Job. In fact, you're just a windbag. You don't fear God. Your words are sinful and crafty, and they themselves condemn you. Besides, you're too young to really know anything. Age and wisdom are on our side. You're being arrogant because of your immaturity."

Lacking new material, Eliphaz then repeats a line from his first speech about sinning angels and weak humans, probably saying it a little louder the second time, as we all tend to do. Cranking up his indignation, Eliphaz no longer sees a potential happy future for Job, and he becomes completely focused on making his point and winning the argument: *"If you will listen, I will show you. I will answer you from my own experience"* (Job 15:17).

The insults continue to flow. Eliphaz accuses Job of trusting in his riches (Job 15:31), assuring him that he must be sinful since *"the godless are barren"* (Job 15:34).

Bildad picks up where Eliphaz leaves off, arrogantly wondering, *"How long before you stop talking?"* (Job 18:2) Two verses later, he essentially asks Job, "Do you think you're so important that your fate is earth-shattering? Bad stuff happens to the wicked all the time." The bulk of his speech then reiterates the alarming fate of the wicked—and he's sure to take another cheap shot at Job's bereavement (Job 18:19).

When Zophar speaks again, he demonstrates that he, in concert with the others, has turned a deaf ear to Job's testimony. As Job pours out his heart for understanding, Zophar takes it as a personal affront. He complains, *"I've had to endure your insults"* (Job 20:3). And having nothing new to say, he says it anyway, proceeding with twenty-six more verses of broken record material regarding the imminent judgment of the wicked in this life (Job 20:4–29).

When Eliphaz delivers his last speech, his moral decline is flagrant. His conclusion is that Job is pure evil: *"There's no limit to your sins"* (Job 22:5). He proceeds to declare Job guilty of ruthless lending practices, depriving starving people of food and water, turning his back on needy widows and orphans, lusting after money, and telling God to mind his own business. This is a far cry from Eliphaz's first speech, when he calmly insinuated that perhaps Job had a little sin in his life.

And when he says, *"The righteous will be happy to see the wicked destroyed, and the innocent will laugh in contempt"* (Job 22:19), one can't help but wonder if Eliphaz himself is laughing at Job under his breath. There is a real tone of gloating in his remarks.

The final speech comes from Bildad, and it's quite short. Mainly, he wants to say two things: God is awesome and humans are awful.

In his words, *"God is powerful and dreadful… In comparison, people are maggots; we mortals are mere worms"* (Job 25:2, 6). And when he says *we*, I think what Bildad really means is *you*—"Job, you are a maggot. Like the maggots crawling in the sores all over your body, you are that insignificant."

By the end, lacking any new insights, the friends lose interest in speaking again with Job: *"Job's three friends refused to reply further to him because he kept insisting on his innocence"* (Job 32:1). In other words, their attitude had come to a cocky final resting place.

They seem to have no concept of genuine and compassionate communication, and they just prod each other on to greater and greater ignorance and boring repetition.

Here is the great irony of the tale. Job, enduring the debate with incredible duress, not only stays the course but improves himself by clinging to God. The friends, sitting pretty with their wealth and good health, are the ones who deteriorate.

This is the opposite of what one would expect.

Without the weight of any personal trial bearing down upon them, the friends become complacent. Their security gives them the false assurance that God is totally pleased with them. Because their lives are comfy, they assume they must be doing things right. With nothing left to figure out, their pride begins to destroy their character. And they get meaner.

Their theology of God's sovereignty has glimpses of brilliance, but it's thin and incomplete. Their spiritual pride, bolstered by their lack of personal connection with God, hardens their hearts. Craving mercy, compassion, and a listening ear, all Job receives is condescension regarding his supposed deception and wickedness.

Well, that's the path the friends took—and it shouldn't surprise us. Left to our own devices, disconnected from God, we can destroy our dignity with some very bad ideas, even when our sentences are full of religious words. History testifies that even the most decent folk can partake in some very nasty activities, given the right circumstances.

On the other hand, Job takes an upward spiritual path. How he does this is both obvious and obscure. Let's consider in more detail how he was able to forge a better course.

At the beginning, it doesn't look like Job is going to make it. His first outburst consists of a desperate cry to end it all. He curses the day of his birth and even the moment of his conception. Job just wants to die. He can't imagine any reason to live, given his level of misery. After verse upon verse of pure wallowing, Job concludes, *"I have no peace, no quietness. I have no rest"* (Job 3:26).

Throughout the early rounds of the debate, Job repeats his gloomy theme song. After Eliphaz first speaks, Job says,

> *I wish he would crush me.*
> > *I wish he would reach out his hand and kill me.*
> *At least I can take comfort in this:*
> > *Despite the pain,*
> *I have not denied the words of the Holy One.*
> *But I don't have the strength to endure.*
> > *I have nothing to live for.*
>
> —Job 6:9–11

He further adds, *"I would rather be strangled—rather die than suffer like this. I hate my life and don't want to go on living"* (Job 7:15–16). And after Bildad's first speech, Job declares to God, *"Why, then, did you deliver me from my mother's womb? Why didn't you let me die at birth? It would be as though I had never existed, going directly from the womb to the grave"* (Job 10:18–19).

But this line of thinking doesn't last. By the time Zophar joins the dialogue, instead of simply pleading for his death, Job laments about the brevity of human life, and even begins to wonder about the possibility of life after death. He contemplates, *"Can the dead live again? If so, this would give me hope through all my years of struggle, and I would eagerly await the release of death"* (Job 14:14).

As woeful as these early death-wish remarks appear, they gradually diminish in Job's discourse, disappearing after the fourteenth chapter. Even though his lament over the degree of suffering never fades, Job's last six speeches are free of his earlier obsession with death.

Furthermore, Job demonstrates a positive progression through his evolving concept of a mediator between God and man. The stages of his thought process illustrate landmarks in his spiritual development.

Responding to the friends' encouragement to take up his cause before God, Job first replies with, *"But how can a person be declared innocent in God's sight? If someone wanted to take God to court, would it be possible to answer him even once in a thousand times?"* (Job 9:2–3)

By the end of this very same chapter, Job is envisioning the existence of a potential arbitrator to work things out with God:

> *If only there were a mediator between us,*
>   *someone who could bring us together.*
> *The mediator could make God stop beating me,*
>   *and I would no longer live in terror of his punishment.*
> *Then I could speak to him without fear,*
>   *but I cannot do that in my own strength.*
>   —Job 9:33–35

The first version of this exchange is somewhat crude, like a referee breaking up a mismatched fight in a sporting event. But before long, Job's concept of a mediator assumes a healthier form.

> *Even now my witness is in heaven.*
>   *My advocate is there on high.*

> *My friends scorn me,*
> > *but I pour out my tears to God.*
> *I need someone to mediate between God and me,*
> > *as a person mediates between friends.*
>
> —Job 16:19–21

By his fifth speech, Job is approaching something that resembles New Testament theology on the matter, even though he knew nothing about the role Jesus would come to play. By his sixth speech, Job hits it out of the park by declaring his belief in a personal redeemer who can rescue him.

> *But as for me, I know that my Redeemer lives,*
> > *and he will stand upon the earth at last.*
> *And after my body has decayed,*
> > *yet in my body I will see God!*
> *I will see him for myself.*
> > *Yes, I will see him with my own eyes.*
> > *I am overwhelmed at the thought!*
>
> —Job 19:25–27

This declaration of faith late in Job's discourse is a far cry from where he started out. His stock is rising.

And speaking of special declarations, one of Job's finest comes in his eighth speech. After asserting that he cannot see God, he declares that he knows God can see him, and that God is in control of his life.

> *But he knows where I am going.*
> > *And when he tests me, I will come out as pure as gold.*
> *For I have stayed on God's paths;*
> > *I have followed his ways and not turned aside.*

> *I have not departed from his commands,*
>> *but have treasured his words more than daily food.*
> *But once he has made his decision, who can change his mind?*
>> *Whatever he wants to do, he does.*
> *So he will do to me whatever he has planned.*
>> *He controls my destiny.*
>
> —Job 23:10–14

Notice how Job at this point believes that God has plans for his life. He no longer wants to die. He's thinking about the future and what God might have in mind for his broken life. It even sounds like Job recognizes his terrible ordeal as a test, run by the sovereign Lord for the purpose of some sort of purification.

And because he has not forsaken the commands of the Lord, Job confidently sees himself as potentially emerging from the test in better shape than he went in, like gold that has been purified in the fire. Things are looking up.

We see more evidence of Job's improving character in the substance of his later utterances. By his eighth speech, he calmly affirms that even though the wicked may prosper in this life, at some point in the future they will receive their judgment (Job 24:22–24). In his ninth speech, responding to Bildad for the last time, Job speaks with confidence of the great power and majesty of God in nature. It is a beautiful poetic utterance with no hint of despair.

In his final discourse, Job waxes eloquently on all sorts of subjects. These later deliberations reveal notable headway in his spiritual maturation. He even boldly declares his friends to be wrong: *"I will maintain my innocence without wavering. My conscience is clear for as long as I live"* (Job 27:6).

In Job 28, he delivers an elegant articulation on the nature and location of true wisdom and understanding:

> *God alone understands the way to wisdom;*
> *he knows where it can be found…*
>
> *And this is what he says to all humanity:*
> *"The fear of the Lord is true wisdom;*
> *to forsake evil is real understanding."*
>
> —Job 28:23, 28

Remarkably, Job is starting to grasp a spiritual truth that wise Solomon would declare years later: if one is ever to acquire true wisdom regarding the complexities of human existence, such understanding begins only with a healthy fear of the Lord. And a healthy fear of the Lord can only begin by abandoning any notion of God as being comparable to an extraordinarily great human. A more colossal view of God as infinite and omnipotent compels one to a posture of reverent fear and submission, to the point of abandoning oneself completely to the love and care of the Creator, regardless of current circumstance.

Amazingly, this is the territory in which Job begins to move.

He then discards his pessimistic fatalism and speaks merrily of his delightful former blessings. Instead of focusing solely on his present pain, Job is able to reminisce about the good old days: *"When I was in my prime, God's friendship was felt in my home"* (Job 29:4).

But Job can't entirely cast off the agony of the moment. The next chapter is best understood as a brief lapse where Job again itemizes the details of his physical suffering and social abandonment. Even though he's making good progress, occasionally he still needs to express his emotions honestly, as all humans are compelled to do in the face of misery that continues to drag on with no light at the end of the tunnel.

Job's tenth speech completes his contribution to the debate. And as he belts out his last hoorah, he makes a final and rather comprehensive case, delivering one last call for God to show himself and address what still feels like injustice: *"Let God weigh me on the scales of justice, for he knows my integrity"* (Job 31:6).

As he makes this final plea to the Almighty regarding his innocence, there is a strength and peace in his words that didn't exist in his earlier remarks. You can feel it when you read them.

Undeniably, Job is becoming a different man. The pain and anguish hasn't subsided, but he's changing on the inside. His theology is deeper and richer. His heart is softer.

And when it comes time to meet God face to face, Job's inner renovation is showcased by two spiritual benchmarks: his enthusiasm to submit fully to the God he loves and his readiness to repent of his sin of presumptuous speech.

His heart and mind have been remodelled. Truly, he has come a long way from the suicidal grief of his first speech.

Job has come this great distance because of the good work of God in his heart. Even though he doesn't realize it in real time, through the excruciating affliction of the journey God transforms Job into a wiser, richer vessel. That transformation occurs because of Job's faith—the faith we saw in full force in the opening scenes of the drama, as well the faith that appears in the form of its messy cousin throughout the meat of the narrative. But faith it is. Faith in God. Job never abandons God, so God never abandons Job.

It is fair to ask: how do we know for sure that it was God's presence in Job's life that allows him to make such great strides? Maybe it was just human resiliency. Maybe Job was born with a uniquely tough hide. Some might argue that the text doesn't explicitly say anything about God quietly working in Job's life throughout the trial.

Even though the record doesn't spell it out in such straightforward terms, there are many reasons to believe that God is largely responsible for Job's positive transformation.

First and foremost, what else could account for his miraculous metamorphosis? What other explanations are even remotely believable? To say that it was purely human resilience is just as unprovable as to say it was God. Besides, humans are prone to despair in the face of extreme tragedy. Initially, Job was hardcore suicidal, and his situation only got worse. To arrive at the amazing place where he eventually lands is clearly a supernatural undertaking.

It would be a farce to say that human tenacity alone explains his improvement. Notice that Job's endurance is based on his belief in a God whom he thinks can help him. As he declares in his final speech, God is the one who brings wisdom to the hearts of humans who fear him. Intellectually, he knows God is imminent; he just can't feel it. Besides, if Job had improved himself spiritually apart from God, it would render the whole story illogical.

Even though this book doesn't say anything specific about God quietly and mysteriously working in the lives of humans, the rest of Scripture does. James 1:17 informs us, *"Every good thing given and every perfect gift is from above"* (NASB). If something good happens in this creation, God is behind it. He's the source of every benevolent aspect of the human experience, from the ability to enjoy a steak to the compassion of a friend. If there is good work happening in Job's spiritual life, its source is God.

Other scriptures are anxious to weigh in on the matter. The writer of Hebrews records God's promise to never fail us or forsake us (Hebrews 13:5). In this life, his constant presence is assured. The psalmist David agrees: *"I can never escape from your Spirit! I can never get away from your presence!"* (Psalm 139:7) In Psalm 23, David also speaks of God as our tender shepherd who leads, guides, and strengthens us, always remaining close when we walk through our darkest valleys. Whether you believe in him, God is doing good work in your life right now

Yes, I think we can be confident that the formidable God described in the Book of Job is the only source of strength that could sustain this saint's stamina. God's compassionate presence rescued

Job from the edge of the abyss and brought him to the beautiful and brilliant orations at the end of the narrative. Job's path was made possible by the goodness of God.

But that is not to say that there was no human resilience involved in the story. There certainly was. By faith, Job clawed his way forward. He knew that God was his only hope, so he never stopped petitioning the Lord for help.

This reflects another part of the paradoxical mystery of God's work in our lives. Commenting on the nature of Christian sanctification in general, the Apostle Paul said in one of his letters to *"work out your own salvation with fear and trembling; for it is God who is at work in you, both to desire and to work for His good pleasure"* (Philippians 2:12–13, NASB).

Work out your salvation. God is at work in you. We work. God works. Both efforts play a part. And the more faith we inject into the situation, the more God is free to release his divine power into our lives.

As the writer James also says, *"Come close to God and He will come close to you"* (James 4:8, NASB).

Job's upward trajectory cannot be considered to be anything less than amazing. What a contrast to the friends' path, wandering around in their own theological wilderness with little divine assistance. Those poor fellows display no spiritual growth, no forward progress whatsoever, all because they were stuck in their flawed perception of God's sovereignty.

As Harold Kushner so aptly said earlier, the friends could only see God as a kindly cosmic vending machine instead of the true Sovereign of the universe that he is, working and willing entirely according to his own good purposes.

Also working against the friends is their absence of personal connection with God. Loving theology more than loving God can lead to arrogance, lack of empathy, and a lot of failed ministry.

Another shortfall with the friends was their failure to appreciate the substantial role one's personal experience plays in consoling those who suffer. If you haven't lived through intense and largely unmerited suffering, be wary of wading into the deep waters of those who have. When your experience lacks but duty calls, exercise humility and a good listening ear.

As an illustration of this last point, consider the following anecdote from the life of C.S. Lewis, a story made famous in the movie *Shadowlands*.

Throughout his speaking tour and in his writings, Lewis regularly presented the following message regarding the role of pain in the Christian's life:

> Pain is God's megaphone to rouse a deaf world. You see, we are like blocks of stone out of which the Sculptor carves the forms of men. The blows of his chisel, which hurt us so much, are what make us perfect.[12]

Using a bit of artistic licence perhaps, the movie's version of this has actor Anthony Hopkins finishing each presentation with the following punchline: "Pain is the chisel the divine sculptor uses to shape us into his people."[13]

As true as that statement may be, it's also far less valuable than one would expect. For as the movie unfolds, we witness a turn of events that alters Lewis's ability to speak confidently about the meaning of suffering.

---

[12] "C.S. Lewis Quotes," *AZ Quotes*. Date of access: August 31, 2020 (https://www.azquotes.com/quote/1385523).

[13] *Shadowlands,* directed by Richard Attenborough (Los Angeles, CA: Savoy Pictures, 1993).

In his fifties, the great theologian establishes a warm and rich relationship with American poet Joy Davidman. The movie depicts the charming nature of their love story.

But quite abruptly the warm scene turns to sadness. After four years of marriage, Lewis tragically loses the love of his life to cancer. The textbook monologue has become real life, and things change for the great orator. His famous one-liner seems less meaningful, less clever, less useful.

To put it succinctly, Lewis was comfortable with his tidy little mantra only until he himself suffered a deep personal tragedy. At that point, he began to acknowledge that much about the suffering of the righteous is a mystery beyond our understanding.

Or as Harold Kushner put it, "In choosing the truth of real life over the comfortable illusion of traditional belief, C.S. Lewis does something Job's friends are incapable of doing."[14]

I would add, in so doing, Lewis became an even more powerful and authentic witness to the majesty and mystery of God.

---

[14] Kushner, *The Book of Job*, 99.

THEOLOGICAL INSIGHTS OF A YOUNG EAVESDROPPER

Anyone who claims the Book of Job is easy to understand is a charlatan. Beware of what they're selling. The dense theological and philosophical issues aroused by the book have challenged the greatest minds of every generation since its composition.

Nevertheless, with time and effort we become more confident responding to some of the puzzling matters in the narrative. Other enigmas, however, have solutions that seem to dance in and out of focus. They temporarily peek out from behind their opaque hiding spots, then quickly resume their blurry aura.

Quite bluntly, some questions in the Book of Job seem to have no clear answers whatsoever. For example, why does Job's adversity have to be so extreme? That's something I don't think I will ever comprehend.

We know a few things for certain.

Firstly, the Book of Job is an impressive treatise on faith. It causes the reader to contemplate the meaning of trusting God fully. To what extent will Job, or any devout believer, serve God for nothing, for no earthly benefit? Are humans capable of remaining faithful to God and giving him the adoration he deserves just because of who he is as opposed to how he might reward them for their piety?

Secondly, the Book of Job creates a lot of space for the laments of hurting souls in the midst of calamity. We must allow them to ask the tough questions. God isn't put off by our passionate honesty, even if bystanders are. As I have said repeatedly, we need to acknowledge that the freedom to ask honest questions offers something powerful in the healing process, something which rote theological answers don't possess—even more so if the theological solutions are delivered in a smug manner.

Thirdly, God's silence doesn't signify his absence. His presence is evident in the life of Job while he suffers, even though Job himself doesn't recognise it at the time. By observing the healthy progress in his thought patterns throughout the course of the debate, we can see that God does good work in the heart of his faithful servant, refining him into a more precious jewel. And God's good work is possible because Job, as angry and frustrated as he is at times, maintains all his focus on his relationship with God. He keeps everything pointed in the right direction.

Fourthly, those who choose to come alongside a suffering fellow traveller must do so with a healthy balance of information and compassion. If love and mercy are lacking, the theological information they impart will be meaningless. God wants people to mourn with those who mourn, not inform those who mourn with great theological prowess. Counsellors must be graciously present with those they counsel. Merely proving oneself right is pretty much useless.

Finally, until we become more comfortable with humbly accepting the paradoxical and mysterious blend of God's sovereignty and goodness, we will forever be frustrated, and probably say a lot of foolish things that hurt people. Undoubtedly, our opinions on this matter are much clearer and more strongly proclaimed when we ourselves have not actually experienced such disproportionate and unjust suffering.

These are some of the things we know for certain. Let's see what else we can pick up as we push towards the finish line.

Once Job and the friends have exhausted every drop of water from their respective wells, the drama takes a turn. As we come to Job 32–37, we meet a new character in the story. Unbeknownst to us, a young theologian named Elihu has been eavesdropping on the debate. Like every spectator so far, he feels compelled to join the discussion. But he isn't happy with what he's heard so far. In fact, he's angry. He thinks all the participants are wrong.

Elihu is angry with Job *"because he justified himself before God"* (Job 32:2, NASB). And he is upset with the friends *"because they had found no answer, and yet had condemned Job"* (Job 32:3, NASB).

As the text will show, Elihu believes Job is out of line, not because he's a secret serial killer but because of the way he has been talking to God. The young eavesdropper thinks Job's companions are out of line because they pronounce judgment on Job without ever answering one of his questions.

Out of respect for their age, Elihu has kept his mouth shut and let the old boys hash it out. But he reaches a breaking point that thrusts him out of his silence. Concluding that the elderly aren't necessarily wiser, Elihu declares that it's his time to speak (Job 32:9–10). In fact, he's about to explode: *"I am full of pent-up words… I am like a cask of wine without a vent, like a new wineskin ready to burst!"* (Job 32:18–19)

Despite his melodramatic entrance, Elihu delivers a plethora of wisdom that both Job and his friends need to hear.

To a certain degree, Elihu arrives on the scene as the negotiator Job has been anticipating. Obviously, he's not the perfect mediator between man and God, but his words contribute well to the cause of establishing a better paradigm of God's sovereignty and goodness. Elihu helps move the dialogue along from its stagnant position at the end of Job 31.

Warning! Elihu can sound a little cocky at times—*"I am a man of great knowledge"* (Job 36:4)—but don't let that detract from the wisdom of his words. His insights are far more helpful than the friends'. Job will be better prepared to meet God face to face after Elihu's theological tutorial.

Because Elihu speaks for five straight chapters once the cork is popped, we cannot cover every detail of his speech. So we'll skim through the passage and highlight some general truths he wants to share with Job. Then we'll do another pass, noting the arguments he presents in defence of his main thesis, a thesis that makes a case for the goodness of God.

But before we get to that, we need to understand Elihu's position on Job's moral standing. Is he guilty or innocent? Unlike the friends who ultimately condemn Job for a surplus of sins, Elihu's main contention concerns the irreverent way Job has been talking to God (Job 34:7). He believes Job has erred by speaking angrily with the Almighty: *"Job, you deserve the maximum penalty for the wicked way you have talked. For you have added rebellion to your sin; you show no respect, and you speak many angry words against God"* (Job 34:36–37).

Unlike the friends, who seem bent on proving themselves to be right, Elihu is concerned for Job's heart and where his anger might take him.

From the outset, Elihu desires to tell Job that he is on his side. He is advocating for him. The young man says, *"Look, you and I both belong to God. I, too, was formed from clay. So you don't need to be afraid of me. I won't come down hard on you"* (Job 33:6–7). He assures Job that he's not putting himself on a pedestal or looking down his nose at him, as the friends did. Elihu proclaims that he and Job are on the same level. His only motivation is to secure a good resolution to Job's tragic situation. He assures Job, *"I am anxious to see you justified"* (Job 33:32).

Contrary to the friends, Elihu seems to have Job's good at heart. Accordingly, he wants Job to know he has been listening to him, carefully: *"You have spoken in my hearing, and I have heard your very words"* (Job 33:8).

Where the friends ignored Job's words and just blathered on, Elihu repeatedly quotes from Job's speeches, at least ten times! Certainly,

Elihu disagrees with much of what Job has said, but he dignifies Job as a person by showing the poor guy that he has been listening.

At this point in the conversation, it's also valuable for Job to start hearing what he himself has been saying, so he can engage in some proper self-reflection.

Another matter troubling Elihu is Job's notion that whenever things go south in our lives, it signifies that God is being mean to us. The young theologian wants Job to know unequivocally that God is never mean to us. As much as Job might have come to see God as his enemy, Elihu says, *"You are wrong…"* (Job 33:12) God is always on our side, and he is always speaking to us in various manners, *"though people do not recognize it"* (Job 33:14). Elihu reassures Job, *"Truly God will not do wrong. The Almighty will not twist justice"* (Job 34:12).

In response to Job's demand for a hearing before God, Elihu says, *"We don't set the time when we will come before God in judgment"* (Job 34:23). He reminds Job that when the oppressed call out to God for justice, he *"hears the cries of the needy"* (Job 34:28). But, Elihu adds, *"if he chooses to remain quiet, who can criticize him?"* (Job 34:29)

Just because we don't like our circumstances, God is not obliged to rearrange his plans and start doing things on our terms. Rhetorically, Elihu drives it home: *"Must God tailor his justice to your demands?"* (Job 34:33)

Along the same line, he chastises Job for claiming that God isn't listening to his cries of despair.

> *But it is wrong to say God doesn't listen,*
> *   to say the Almighty isn't concerned.*
> *You say you can't see him,*
> *   but he will bring justice if you will only wait.*
> *You say he does not respond to sinners with anger*
> *   and is not greatly concerned about wickedness.*

> *But you are talking nonsense, Job.*
> *You have spoken like a fool.*
>
> —Job 35:13–16

Elihu adds that Job is disproportionately preoccupied with the prosperity of the wicked, those sinners who continue to do well without facing the immediate judgment of God. In his words, *"But you are obsessed with whether the godless will be judged. Don't worry, judgment and justice will be upheld"* (Job 36:17). Instead of this silly fixation on what's going to happen to other people, Elihu warns Job to stay focused on his own heart and its propensity to sin: *"But watch out, or you may be seduced by wealth"* (Job 36:18).

Furthermore, Elihu wants Job to grasp the true nature of God's transcendence. In the ebb and flow of human life and hardship, we must remember who God is.

As I've said before, and Elihu reiterates in his own way, God is not just a really good human. He's so big and beyond us that he can never be impacted by our behaviour, whether good or bad. Elihu explains,

> *If you sin, how does that affect God?*
> *Even if you sin again and again,*
> *what effect will it have on him?*
> *If you are good, is this some great gift to him?*
> *What could you possibly give him?*
> *No, your sins affect only people like yourself,*
> *and your good deeds also affect only humans.*
>
> —Job 35:6–8

God's transcendence, his empathetic listening ear, his desire and ability to eventually bring all human life to justice… these themes are important to Elihu. But by far the most significant thing Elihu wants to say to his fellow theologians is that God is a good God of love.

Many people who read the Book of Job wonder how God can be considered good while allowing his faithful servant Job to suffer so severely. As if anticipating this question among future believers, Elihu makes a strong case for a loving God who is always good. He defends Yahweh as an all-powerful God who is continually and compassionately working for the good of all.

As Elihu has already declared, we aren't doing God any favours by being good. He doesn't need us, nor can we impact him by our behaviour. On the contrary, God is perpetually doing *us* favours through his miraculous and benevolent power.

Whatever else Elihu may be saying, most certainly he is calling for all the parties involved in this story to be brought back to the one pure and simple truth that God is good, all the time.

Elihu provides numerous examples to prove his point.

At the most basic level, he says that God shows his goodness to us by giving us life through his spirit, and by sustaining that life with his breath.

> *But there is a spirit within people,*
> *the breath of the Almighty within them,*
> *that makes them intelligent.*
>
> —Job 32:8

> *If God were to take back his spirit*
> *and withdraw his breath,*
> *all life would cease,*
> *and humanity would turn again to dust.*
>
> —Job 34:14–15

Elihu says that God is good because he gives us the marvellous gift of life, sustaining it daily.

Secondly, God is good to us by giving us the advantage of an incredible mind. As we just read, it is God's spirit that makes us intelligent. Elihu builds on this by referring to God as *"the one who makes us smarter than the animals and wiser than the birds of the sky"* (Job 35:11). Our complex brain structure, with its high-performing intellectual capacity, is a kind gift from God. It's a manifestation of his goodness to us.

As well, God displays his goodness by speaking to us through our conscience, warning us and protecting us from the ravages of sin. In response to Job's lament over God's supposed silence, Elihu explains,

> *For God speaks again and again,*
> > *though people do not recognize it.*
> *He speaks in dreams, in visions of the night,*
> > *when deep sleep falls on people*
> > *as they lie in their beds.*
> *He whispers in their ears*
> > *and terrifies them with warnings.*
> *He makes them turn from doing wrong;*
> > *he keeps them from pride.*
> *He protects them from the grave,*
> > *from crossing over the river of death.*
>
> —Job 33:14–18

We need to recognize our conscience as a wonderful gift from God. Because our hearts are so naturally deceitful and desperately wicked, thank God for his loving nudge that repeatedly works to put us back on the right path.

Similarly, God is good to us by occasionally disciplining us with hardships or illness to move us toward repentance of our sin.

> Or God disciplines people with pain on their sickbeds,
> > with ceaseless aching in their bones.
> They lose their appetite
> > for even the most delicious food.
> Their flesh wastes away,
> > and their bones stick out…
>
> When he prays to God,
> > he will be accepted.
> And God will receive him with joy
> > and restore him to good standing.
> He will declare to his friends,
> "I sinned and twisted the truth,
> > but it was not worth it."
>
> —Job 33:19–21, 26–27

When we ignore God's voice in our conscience, he's prepared to up the ante and lay us out to get our full attention. Expressing it another way, Elihu adds, *"But by means of their suffering, he rescues those who suffer. For he gets their attention through adversity"* (Job 36:15). God's commitment to our holiness is a strong demonstration of his love for us.

Elihu also wants the old boys to know that God proves his goodness to us by saving us from sin's curse and giving us true life. In his words, *"He rescues them from the grave so they may enjoy the light of life"* (Job 33:30). Every inkling of sin in life is detrimental, resulting in some form of death. Sin kills peace, trust, relationships, everything. But God in his goodness wants to give us true life—not just the ability to have a heartbeat, but the opportunity to experience the fountain of living water within God himself.

Furthermore, God illustrates his goodness to us though his masterful creation. Rhetorically, and perhaps sarcastically, Elihu asks, *"Did someone else put the world in his care? Who set the whole world in place?"* (Job 34:13) Apart from everything else that may be out there in our vast universe, this planet alone is truly remarkable. Did God have to make it so diversely beautiful? Was he dutybound to load it up with such rich resources? Was he obliged to give us the joys of seasonal variety, with a sun that heats and energizes the entire operation so effortlessly? No, he could have made it bland, boring, and utilitarian. But he didn't. He made it so sensational because he is good, and he loves us.

Elihu then goes on to assert that God demonstrates his goodness by bringing us comfort in our times of need or trial. At one point in his argument, Elihu refers to the Creator God as *"the one who gives songs in the night"* (Job 35:10).

Countless are the testimonies of those who have experienced God's goodness amidst their darkest hour. When our oldest daughter was diagnosed with cancer in 2010, I will never forget the peace God gave to our hearts as we navigated that dark valley. I'll always remember the way he miraculously sang his songs of love into our broken hearts. God is good because he comforts us in our sorrows.

Additionally, Elihu argues that God exhibits his goodness by being more gracious to us than he needs to be. The young theologian affirms, *"God is mighty, but he does not despise anyone!"* (Job 36:5) He goes on to say, *"We cannot imagine the power of the Almighty; but even though he is just and righteous, he does not destroy us"* (Job 37:23).

In the secular world, humans with a lot of power often abuse their strength. God in his great might and holiness would be justified in dealing harshly with us as flawed, fallen creatures. But because God is good, his first response is to operate out of grace.

Moreover, God displays his goodness toward us by always working for our greater good. Analyzing Job's situation, Elihu concludes, *"God is leading you away from danger, Job, to a place free from distress. He is setting your table with the best food"* (Job 36:16). The best food?

These words may confuse us, as they undoubtedly did Job. But Elihu is convinced that God is on a mission for Job's greater good. Listen to his summary statement on the matter: *"for God sent this suffering to keep you from a life of evil"* (Job 36:21).

As confusing as present conditions may be, a heart of faith believes that God is always sovereignly working for our good, unceasingly absorbed with our best interests.

Moving from the realm of the intangible to the physical world, Elihu asserts that God showcases his goodness through the earth's water cycle. As an illustration of God's benevolent power, Elihu kicks into meteorological mode: *"He draws up the water vapor and then distills it into rain. The rain pours down from the clouds, and everyone benefits"* (Job 36:27–28). He adds, *"By these mighty acts he nourishes the people, giving them food in abundance"* (Job 36:31).

Referencing God's resume of his mighty work in nature, Elihu exhorts Job, *"Stop and consider the wonderful miracles of God!"* (Job 37:14)

What greater illustration of God's kindness do we need? The miraculous water cycle has been designed entirely for our benefit, and ultimately for our dining pleasure as we daily enjoy its produce.

Finally, Elihu contends that God is even good to us by protecting us from the scorching power of the hot sun.

> *Do you understand how he moves the clouds*
> *with wonderful perfection and skill?*
> *When you are sweltering in your clothes*
> *and the south wind dies down and everything is still,*
> *he makes the skies reflect the heat like a bronze mirror.*
> —Job 37:16–18

We could keep going, but Elihu has made his point. The weight of Job's suffering and the discouragement of the friends' cruelty tempted him to doubt God's goodness. At that point, along came a feisty young man who spoke healing truth into the troubled and confused minds of his elders. Elihu assured the old guys that God is never mean in the way humans perceive malice. He is loving and good to all, the righteous and the wicked. And he demonstrates that goodness toward us continually, in so many ways.

While the three friends say nice things about God in their speeches, their paradigm is too narrow. To them, God's only concern is to make the righteous rich and comfortable, and the wicked miserable and dead. Elihu, on the other hand, sees God as more complex. He presents a picture of God more fully in his true splendour, as a loving Creator who has good purposes for his creation. Instead of just a good beatdown, Elihu sees God disciplining sinners so that they may come to repentance and *"enjoy the light of life,"* as he calls it.

In Job's case, Elihu concludes that the Almighty has been disciplining Job for the sake of godly development, not punishing him for overt sins he has committed and hidden away. God's purposes are that Job might have an even more glorious future. Such a perspective sounds eerily familiar to the paradoxical words of Jesus in the Gospel of John: *"He cuts off every branch of mine that doesn't produce fruit, and he prunes the branches that do bear fruit so they will produce even more"* (John 15:2).

Elihu accepts that it has been very difficult for Job, but he wants to steer him away from his anger and help him perceive God properly as a God of love, one who performs good work through every one of his acts. Even when his providence is confusing or mysterious, a person of true faith will believe, and probably more readily see, that God always has our good in mind.

In his concluding remarks, Elihu celebrates God's great power and dazzling splendour. He finishes with these simple words: *"No wonder people everywhere fear him. All who are wise show him reverence"* (Job 37:24).

This is the heart of the message Elihu wants to communicate to Job. No matter how tough your present circumstances may be, show God the reverence he deserves. For he is good and he is working for your good.

And judging by Job's immediate willingness to offer up repentance when God finally does appear, it is apparent that our grief-stricken protagonist listened very attentively to Elihu. He got the message, loud and clear.

A WHIRLWIND OF AN ENCOUNTER

As we approach the final chapters of the book, the narrative becomes downright mesmerizing. Job finally gets his wish—an appointment with God himself. Imagine: answers straight from the source. Surely this encounter will provide the solution for all of Job's troubles and confusion.

So far, we've largely seen an impatient Job, one who curses the day he was born, accuses God of treating him unfairly, and demands an accounting from his Maker. With his faith suspended by a thread, his frustration level climaxes: *"Let the Almighty answer me"* (Job 31:35).

But to our hero's surprise, the encounter doesn't go at all as he expected.

When God appears to Job out of the whirlwind, he makes no mention of Job's suffering, engages in no discussion regarding the theology of evil, and doesn't directly respond to any of Job's questions. Instead of God being on the witness stand, answering Job's questions, the roles are reversed. Job is confronted with a mind-numbing inquisition regarding the nature and scope of God's creation. More than seventy items are on the agenda as Job is obliged to drink from the fire hose. The suffering saint who had plenty to say for twenty chapters is rendered speechless.

God's format prompts us to add a couple more questions to our list. Is God's response an appropriate reply to Job's predicament?

And considering that God never answers any of Job's concerns, why in the end is Job satisfied with what God had to say?

Job 38:1 tells us, *"Then the Lord answered Job from the whirlwind…"* In Scripture, God's appearances are often accompanied by storms, demonstrating the terror of the occasion. Anticipating a full vindication with an apology perhaps, Job instead receives a monster science quiz on God's creative power.

But before the quiz, a summary rebuke from God: *"Who is this that questions my wisdom with such ignorant words?"* (Job 38:2) Or, according to the New American Standard Bible, *"Who is this that darkens the divine plan by words without knowledge?"* Optimistically, this opening reprimand from God carries a hint of vindication for Job. He confirms that Job's error was only in his speech, not in the endless list of personal and social crimes the friends were trying to pin on him by the end of their debate.

But the indictment is quite severe. By questioning God's justice and portraying the Lord as his enemy, Job has portrayed God's sovereign design as erroneous or shady. By his presumptuous criticism, Job darkens rather than sheds light on God's plans. Such foolish activity is based on *"words without knowledge,"* says God.

Job has no idea about the debate that occurred in heaven. He wrongly presumes that his suffering implies that God is unhappy with him. And he also lacks a true understanding of God's sovereign power in creation.

Hence, the need for a full and speedy education: *"Brace yourself like a man, because I have some questions for you, and you must answer them"* (Job 38:3). Dumbfounded and likely in shock, Job's heartrate accelerates as he vainly tries to prepare for the unexpected—a list of inquiries so fast and furious that he has no opportunity to even respond.

Here's a condensed version of what we read in Job 38–39: "Where were you, Job, when I created the earth from the ground up, or when I established the boundaries of the mighty oceans? Have you ever orchestrated a sunrise, explored underwater springs, or discovered the depths of the seas? Do you know where the doors of death are located? Do you even know where light and darkness come from? But of course you do; you've been around as long as I have, being such a wise old man. How about my world of precipitation—have you visited my depots of snow and hail, or seen where I store the east wind? Can you tell me who coordinates the behaviour of the rain, dew, ice, and frost? Can you direct the movement of the stars in the sky, forming or destroying constellations? Do you know the physical laws of the universe, and can you use them to control the earth? Who is it that gives living creatures intuition and instinct? Can you command the clouds to send forth her lightning and the rains to soften the parched ground? Are you even able to count all the clouds in the sky, Job?"

From cosmology, oceanography, meteorology, and astronomy, God then moves on to zoology: "Hey Job, can you stalk the prey for a lioness to feed her cubs, or provide food for hungry ravens? Do you know all about the gestation periods of wild goats and deer? Was it you who gave the wild donkey its freedom to escape the noise of the city and seek out pastureland in the mountains? Can you tame a wild ox and have him sleep with you in your room or harvest your crops? Do you know why ostriches have such strange behaviours or why they can run faster than a horse? Have you given the horse his strength and his natural instincts to be such a fierce war animal, having no fear in battle? Is it your wisdom that makes the hawks soar so high or the eagles build their nest in the rocky crags of the high cliffs? Tell me, Job, are we done yet or do you want to keep arguing? You seem quite happy to have become my critic, but can you answer even one of my simple questions?"

As God pauses to take a breath, Job jumps in with the biggest humble hip-waders he can muster.

> *Then Job replied to the Lord, "I am nothing—how could I ever find the answers? I will cover my mouth with my hand. I have said too much already. I have nothing more to say."*
>
> —Job 40:3–5

Here's my guess as to what Job was thinking at this point: "I'm so sorry. I was way out of line. But I get it now and I think we're done here. You've made your point very well and I know it's time for me to shut my mouth and never criticize you again. Thank you so much for showing up. It's been a wild ride, but I think I've learned my lesson."

But it's God, not Job, who decides when the tutorial is over.

> *Brace yourself like a man,*
> > *because I have some questions for you,*
> > *and you must answer them.*
>
> *Will you discredit my justice*
> > *and condemn me just to prove you are right?*
>
> *Are you as strong as God?*
> > *Can you thunder with a voice like his?*
>
> *All right, put on your glory and splendor,*
> > *your honor and majesty.*
>
> *Give vent to your anger.*
> > *Let it overflow against the proud.*
>
> *Humiliate the proud with a glance;*
> > *walk on the wicked where they stand.*
>
> *Bury them in the dust.*
> > *Imprison them in the world of the dead.*
>
> *Then even I would praise you,*
> > *for your own strength would save you.*
>
> —Job 40:8–14

Again, please indulge me as I paraphrase: "Okay Job, do you really perceive you and me to be on the same level? Do you have my strength? Does your voice thunder like mine? If so, why don't you clothe yourself in your glorious garments of splendour and start dealing out some of that angry justice you're so consumed with? Go find everyone you consider to be proud or wicked—you know, those guys who make you jealous because you think their lives are undeservedly better than yours—and just wale on them! Have at 'er. And then, once you've humiliated and smoked these bad guys, relegating them to the grave, we can sit down together and toast your awesome majesty. While we're at it, we'll also celebrate the fact that you have so much power that you can even save yourself!"

Are you surprised by God's deliberate use of sarcasm? Are you uncomfortable with it? Does he behave in a way you think he shouldn't? Does he behave in a way you think you wouldn't? Maybe that's the point. God refuses to be the diluted deity we want him to be.

When will we ever learn? He's not just an extremely good human who has to live up to our expectations of excellent human behaviour. He's not to be judged by any human standard. He is so far beyond us, and we are not in charge of his agenda. We cannot make God do our bidding, no matter how much we think justice and righteousness are on our side. God will be who he wants to be. He will do what he wants to do, and no one can prevent his will.

To further illustrate the mystery of his sovereign power and profound creative mind, the Lord proceeds to give a lengthy description of two incredibly exotic specimens in his creative repertoire, Behemoth and Leviathan.

> *Take a look at Behemoth,*
> *which I made, just as I made you.*
> *It eats grass like an ox.*

> *See its powerful loins*
> > *and the muscles of its belly.*
> *Its tail is as strong as a cedar.*
> > *The sinews of its thighs are knit tightly together.*
> *Its bones are tubes of bronze.*
> > *Its limbs are bars of iron.*
> *It is a prime example of God's handiwork,*
> > *and only its Creator can threaten it.*
> *The mountains offer it their best food,*
> > *where all the wild animals play.*
> *It lies under the lotus plants,*
> > *hidden by the reeds in the marsh.*
> *The lotus plants give it shade*
> > *among the willows beside the stream.*
> *It is not disturbed by the raging river,*
> > *not concerned when the swelling Jordan rushes around it.*
> *No one can catch it off guard*
> > *or put a ring in its nose and lead it away.*
> > > —Job 40:15–24

Some have taken Behemoth to be a mythical beast or dinosaur from the ancient past. But it's quite possible God is just talking about a hippopotamus, a big and strong animal who eats grass and hangs out in the water. The only confusing line is the one that says, *"Its tail is as strong as a cedar"* (Job 40:17). Even then, there are many challenges in the translation of that verse. The New American Standard Bible, for instance, renders this verse a different way: *"He hangs his tail like a cedar,"* which could aptly describe that part of a hippo's anatomy.

Regardless, God is drawing Job's attention to the fact that he created this powerful animal just like he created every human. And this beast can be controlled only by its Maker. No raging river can move it, nor can anyone put a ring in its nose and lead it where they want to go.

Hippos remain largely untameable by humans and are considered the most dangerous terrestrial animal on the African continent, being responsible for the deaths of almost three thousand people every year. Though weighing more than three thousand pounds, they can run at speeds higher than eighteen kilometres per hour.

God wants Job to understand that this marvellous creature is part of his mighty handiwork.

As is Leviathan. The identification of Leviathan is placed by some within the realm of mythical sea monsters or dragons, particularly because of the reference to fire coming out of its mouth and smoke from its nostrils (Job 41:19–20). Creation accounts in ancient Near East literature include the tale of Lotan, a seven-headed sea monster that was defeated by the Canaanite god before he first formed heaven and earth.

But if we assume the fire-breathing aspect to be metaphorical, it is quite conceivable that God is simply talking about the crocodile.

He begins by asking Job, *"Can you catch Leviathan with a hook or put a noose around its jaw?… Will it beg you for mercy or implore you for pity?"* (Job 41:1, 3) Broadening the satire, God adds, *"Will it agree to work for you, to be your slave for life? Can you make it a pet like a bird, or give it to your little girls to play with?"* (Job 41:4–5)

In the thirty-four-verse description of this wild beast, God showcases its untameable nature, fierce teeth, brute strength, and tough, armour-like hide. When he refers to Leviathan making *"the water boil with its commotion"* (Job 41:31), one can picture the harrowing sight of a croc rolling wildly as it incapacitates its prey in its mighty jaws.

But how are hippos and crocodiles even remotely related to Job's situation? Part of the answer lies in the immediate text. In the middle of God's Leviathan lecture, he says, *"And since no one dares to* disturb it, who then can stand up to me? Who has given me anything that I need to pay back? Everything under heaven is mine" (Job 41:10–11).

Essentially, God is telling Job, "If humans are no match for these powerful creatures I whip up in my spare time, how in the world would you ever challenge me, the Creator of all? I'm not in debt to anyone. I don't owe you any explanations, Job. Everything under heaven belongs to me. I made it all, and I will do whatever my will inclines me to do. There's nothing you can do about it."

And to this Job responds, "Oh my! I think you're being very arbitrary and capricious."

Well, no. That's what we might say in a moment of faithlessness. Instead Job says,

> *I know that you can do anything,*
>   *and no one can stop you.*
> *You asked, "Who is this that questions my wisdom with such ignorance?"*
>   *It is I—and I was talking about things I knew nothing about,*
>   *things far too wonderful for me.*
> *You said, "Listen and I will speak!*
>   *I have some questions for you,*
> *and you must answer them."*
> *I had only heard about you before,*
>   *but now I have seen you with my own eyes.*
> *I take back everything I said,*
>   *and I sit in dust and ashes to show my repentance.*
>
>   —Job 42:2–6

As offensive as it may sound to the secular ear, Job is put in his place before God. In contrast to the Sovereign's wisdom and power, Job is shown to be ignorant and impotent. In the words of biblical commentator Roy Zuck, "If he could not comprehend or control God's government in nature, how could he hope to comprehend or control the Lord's ways with man."[15] God doesn't need the help or advice of impatient and ignorant mortals to control the world any more than he needed them to create it.

Contemplating the magnificence of God's reign over all creation, Job appreciates anew the unlimited depths of the Lord's wisdom, majesty, and omnipotence. Faced with the radiant splendour present in every corner of creation, Job is compelled to acknowledge and proclaim Yahweh's absolute power: "God, you can do anything, and I didn't know what I was talking about." In the words of Wesley Morriston,

> Job is confronted with sheer transcendence; he is reminded of the chasm that lies between Creator and creature, and forced to take into account the infinite difference between God's point of view and ours. Job's experience is a breathtaking vision of the inexorable Source and End of all things.[16]

This vision transforms Job into a new person, and his final repentance contains perhaps the most life-changing lines in the book: *"I had only heard about you before, but now I have seen you with my own eyes"* (Job 42:5). Before God's appearance, Job had known God only by report. He and his friends thought of God only in terms of the traditional ideas that were circulating in their contemporary culture.

Now that Job has seen God with his own eyes, "now that he has encountered the God who is really God—all those conventional ideas drop away, and with them Job's complaint against God."[17]

---

[15] Roy Zuck, *Job* (Chicago, IL: Moody Press, 1978), 164.
[16] Wesley Morriston, "God's Answer to Job," *Religious Studies*, September 1996, 356.
[17] Ibid., 352.

Theological activity largely consists of intellectual contemplation, abstract thoughts that inform and enlighten. This is the domain where we process our complaints against God.

True religion, on the other hand, is a life-altering encounter with God. In this realm, we're more inclined to marvel at his beauty than grumble about his failure to deliver us our own personal Camelot. When we experience his presence in a more personal fashion, we are nourished.

Up to this point in time, Job has just been reading the menu. Now he's having dinner. The splendour of God's presence completely changes his worldview.

Only when he encounters God personally is Job finally able to let go of all that he has lost. Compared to what he has seen, his former wealth and social position, even his health and his children, sink into comparative insignificance. Or, in the words of Harold Kushner,

> Job's questions have been answered, his doubts have been erased not [as much] by the content of God's words from the whirlwind but by the contact [itself]. He has met God and all theological quibbles have melted away.[18]

Demonstrating a willingness to surrender all previous demands, Job declares all his bold pronouncements to be foolish spouting. That level of humility was required to recognize that God hadn't come down to explain himself or answer Job's questions. No situation could arise that would warrant a human putting God on the hotseat.

By the conspicuous absence of any reference to human beings in God's science lesson, Job gets the subtle but sobering message that it's not all about him. He has value, but he is a very small piece in God's very big creation puzzle. Think about it—God is so involved in

---

[18] Kushner, *The Book of Job*, 157.

the care of nature's vastness that he even brings rain to places where nobody lives (Job 38:26).

Job starts to get the picture of a very big God who can never be placed under the microscope of human scrutiny. He sees the need to change his thinking, to repent.

But of what does Job repent? Surely not the charges of his friends. No, not at all. Instead we see Job repenting of three things—his proud rebellion, his bold insistence that God must respond to him, and his call for the Almighty to smarten up and correct his ways. Job then admits to sinning in response to his suffering, not to suffering because he sinned.

Because of the ancient nature of the text, and the number of unfamiliar Hebrew words found only in the Book of Job, translation of these phrases can be difficult at times. Some have taken the words of Job's repentance to be a celebration of comfort. Linguist Stephen Mitchell says that the word we translate in the text as "repent" has as its root the Hebrew word *nahem*, which means, most commonly, "to comfort." In fact, it is used ten times in the Book of Job, he says, and it means "to comfort" every time, never "to repent."[19]

If that is the case, another possible translation of Job's confession could be rendered, "I retract, and I am comforted about being mortal." Or, paraphrased more fully, "I reject (everything that has been said to this point by me and my visitors) and (having met God and been assured that I am not alone and abandoned in this world) I am comforted, vulnerable human being that I am."[20] Either translation of the text gives us a consistent view of a humbled man, one who now sees himself and his circumstances properly, one who is now ready to let God be God.

In the past, Job's theology had no room for severe physical or psychological affliction in the life of a godly person. Such a scenario

---

[19] Ibid., 159–160. For example, see Job 6:10, 7:13, 16:2, and 21:34.
[20] Ibid., 160.

would imply that God was acting unjustly. Job's view has been refurbished by his encounter with the Almighty. God's presence, and the words he has spoken, not only transform Job's impression of God's wisdom and power, but also display what Job previously doubted—God's providential care.

Job is not alone. The ship is not lost at sea. The good captain is at the helm. God is competently running and compassionately taking care of his creation, including Job's personal itinerary. Job now sees that the events of his life aren't the product of a fatalistic pinball machine. The degree of his discomfort has been incredible, but his odyssey of agony has not come about because of bad luck. Nor has it been the product of random chaos. There is meaning to what he once deemed madness.

Job now believes that his suffering has been allowed by God for purposes which only the Lord understands. And these purposes are good. Though still hard to fully fathom, Elihu's words are starting to make sense: *"God is leading you away from danger, Job, to a place free from distress. He is setting your table with the best food"* (Job 36:16).

Even though the rapid rounds of divine questioning have felt stressful, Job comes out of it more relaxed. Knowing what he now knows, the pain is less traumatic. The tension begins to release from his shoulders. He can see himself coming to land in a more agreeable place. The pain of his affliction may still be there, but the shock is gone.

Job is, so to speak, put in his place. But the Lord's reprimand shows him that God is kind and loving. His whirlwind appearance demonstrates that he is interested in communicating with man, and in being known personally and intellectually.

This personal, profound knowledge of the divine brings three truths into sharper focus: the finiteness of man in comparison to

God, the futility of bringing complaints against God, and the true satisfaction that comes from man's communion with God.[21]

---

[21] Zuck, *Job*, 185.

HOW THE STORY ENDS/BEGINS

Job's encounter with God's perfect storm is unlike anything he envisioned. When God appears in the whirlwind, he doesn't answer any of Job's questions. He doesn't explain the reason for Job's misery, nor does he even allude to what we might call the problem of evil. Instead of explaining his moral rule in the universe, God uses dozens of rhetorical questions to proclaim the greatness of his creative power. Surprisingly, that's good enough for Job. He is satisfied.

Job declares that he has nothing more to say. He assumes a posture of humble submission before God and feels ashamed of the accusations he made against him. Job asks that they be stricken from the record and then proceeds to repent of his impertinently sinful speech: *"I was talking about things I knew nothing about, things far too wonderful for me"* (Job 42:3).

In other words, Job gets it by admitting that he doesn't get it. He cannot answer any of God's questions, for the Lord himself and his ways are so far beyond anything he can comprehend.

Likewise, we too must assume a posture of extreme humility if we hope to even get in the ballpark of beginning to understand the transcendent component of God's nature. If we cannot embrace Job's God, this mysterious God of love and total sovereignty, we are not worshipping the God of the Bible. We are worshipping a false deity we have created in our own image—a fantastic human, an extraordinarily good version of ourselves.

Job's traditional concept of God collapses because it is too small. It cannot bear the weight of reality. The full magnitude of the Almighty changes Job's perspective of God's providence. Even if the system doesn't work nicely with a clean mechanism of moral justice, Job is okay with that. The only meaningful way forward for him is to submit every facet of his being to the loving, sovereign care of God.

Job's earthly problems begin to diminish as he realizes the true enormity of God. After seeing the Lord personally and hearing him speak, nothing else matters. No more explanations are needed, which leads one to conclude that the Book of Job doesn't so much set out to answer the problem of suffering, but to proclaim a God so great that no answer is needed, for it would transcend the finite mind if given.

With those summary remarks tucked away for further reflection, we now turn to the conclusion of the story.

The first order of business is to consider who else besides Job witnessed God speaking out of the whirlwind. Did Elihu hear it? Were the three friends also in the audience? A natural reading of the text leads one to believe they might have been.

> *After the Lord had finished speaking to Job, he said to Eliphaz the Temanite: "I am angry with you and your two friends, for you have not spoken accurately about me, as my servant Job has."*
> —Job 42:7

Regardless of whether the friends were present, some massive repentance is still in order. God commands the three friends to assemble a hefty sacrifice of fourteen large animals—this is serious—and get Job to act as their priest. The friends are directed to burn the animals as a sin offering while Job provides a prayer of intercession on their behalf. If they obey, God promises to accept Job's prayer and grant them forgiveness. Their act of contrition will secure their safety and ensure that God won't treat them as they deserve.

The nuance of this scene is intriguing. In response to Job's repentance on the heels of his appointment with God, the Lord commands him to go and pray for the three nastiest people in his world. Apparently, Job's load has not yet become lighter, but he participates willingly with no guarantee of a deliverance from his ongoing valley of anguish. There is no indication that he saw the intercession for his friends as a free pass to a better life. He just obeys God.

Wisely, the friends waste no time. They do exactly as they're told, approaching Job with cap in hand, I presume.

One cannot help but notice the irony. Earlier, Zophar had said God was going easy on Job, not giving him half of what he deserved (Job 11:6). No doubt Zophar is now grateful that God isn't giving him what *he* deserves.

Even though our hero is still experiencing a world of hurt, Job's readiness to intercede for his accusers is a further testament to the man's godly character. As is the fact that God refers to him as "my servant" four times. What a beautiful expression of love this is, for Job belongs to the Almighty and is employed in his service.

But what about those verdicts? As we read in the narrative, we are obliged to sort out the final rulings God pronounces upon the characters in the story. Why is Job commended for right speech while the friends are condemned for improper speech? What wrong things did the friends say about God? Have they not been defending his justice? Did they not speak eloquently of his power? Was it not Job who questioned the Lord's justice? And how could God lead Job toward repentance for speaking *"words without knowledge"* (Job 38:2), and then refer to him as the one who spoke the truth?

We find our best answers by contrasting the theories of divine sovereignty embraced by each player.

To uphold their faulty human perception of a just God, the friends imposed limits on his sovereignty. Quite simply, it's wrong to declare that God always and immediately rewards good behaviour and punishes bad behaviour in the moment. This world is fallen. Life is not a storybook that repeatedly deals out reward and retribution in real time. God's sovereign reign certainly goes far beyond such notions of clockwork predictability. The friends' insistent false claims were attempts to box in God, to make him into *their* image instead of the other way around. Consequently, the friends refused to budge from their version of the story, saying, in essence, "We fully understand everything about God's conduct. He can only act in this one way! And by the way, Job, because things are going well for us right now, we know we're right."

On the other hand, Job holds to a concept of God that is much denser. Job's Sovereign is more mysterious in how he works—and more personal. This richer mindset sustained Job through his unspeakable stress. The entire time, Job maintained that his grief-stricken predicament was not God's punishment for some grotesque sin.

This is clearly the right thing to say about God. All in all, Job's concept of God is bigger than that of the friends. And in this matter, bigger is truly better.

Job sees God as totally in charge of the master plan. He believes that God is responsible for his suffering but wrestles with the mystery of why God would allow this to happen to an upright person. And in the deliberation of the verdicts, Job's wrestling with the mysteries of God's divine providence trumps the presumptuous arrogance of the friends.

Furthermore, although Job questions God's justice, chastises him for his silence, and probably says way too many words in general, he comes full circle. Pursuing an intimate connection with the Almighty, Job's speech improves. Then, upon meeting God, he willingly repents of all his sinful assertions.

Certainly, Job's post-whirlwind confession contributes to his verdict of having spoken rightly about God, especially if the friends also heard God speak out of the whirlwind but made no effort on their own to repent of their sins. Not only were the three amigos guilty of defending a defective view of God, they were also liable for treating their friend cruelly while he suffered.

So with the verdicts sorted out, all that remains are the details of Job's restoration. We cannot help but notice the timing. It feels significant: *"When Job prayed for his friends, the Lord restored his fortunes"* (Job 42:10).

It's tempting to say that God rewards Job *because* Job prays for and most likely forgives his friends. But if this were true, we might in turn be tempted to promise others relief from their suffering if they similarly practice some intercessory prayer. Sorry. No such formula exists.

To remain true to the theology of the book, we cannot consider Job's restoration to be an automatic prize for being godly, or in this case for being a righteous and forgiving prayer warrior. If that were the case, the friends were right all along. Which, of course, we know they weren't. God doesn't sit there with prizes in hand, waiting to reward every good deed done by humans.

Obviously it didn't hurt Job's case before God that he did the right things, that he hung in there throughout the trial, repented of the sins of his mouth when reprimanded, and forgave and prayed for his friends when called upon to do so. Job did some very good deeds. But we must consider the restored fortunes that come his way to be tokens of God's grace, not paid-for candy bars from the divine cosmic vending machine. At this point in the story, God freely and sovereignly bestowed his goodness upon Job. He wasn't obliged to reward his servant's piety.

Now, don't get me wrong: the Book of Job does not deny the general rule found repeatedly in Scripture, that God blesses the righteous. Take, for example, what we read in Psalm 5:12: *"For you bless the godly, O Lord; you surround them with your shield of love"*—or the words of Solomon: *"The righteous will be rewarded with prosperity"* (Proverbs

13:21, NASB). This is clearly a general principle within the divine order, something that's present in God's good creation.

But early in the story of divine revelation, God includes a qualifier on the promise—he does not bless righteous behaviour with a fixed formula. There is no recipe that causes a perfect blessing cake to come out of the oven every time. In fact, God often blesses the lives of the wicked alongside the righteous. Truly, God by his sovereignty can withhold or bestow his blessings on whomever he chooses for purposes known only to him.

In this case, God chose to honour Job in a manner that outshone his first round of blessings. Some things were doubled—wealth, livestock, and the years of life perhaps. While some fortunes were doubled, other were replaced but with better quality: restored and likely deeper relationships with his friends and family who had abandoned him earlier, gifts of money and gold rings as tokens of comfort, and ten more children with daughters who were remarkable in beauty and heritage. Their special qualities even granted them the honour of being named in the text while the sons remain anonymous, rather uncommon in that culture.

Nevertheless, the story then ends abruptly: *"Then he died, an old man who had lived a long, full life"* (Job 42:17). That's an understatement.

In place of juicy details, our imaginations run wild with speculation as we fill in the missing pieces of this fascinating story. In the second phase of Job's life, what was the nature of his relationship with his three friends? Did he still have the same wife, and did she bear him these ten new children? How did Job describe his experience to curious inquirers? Did God and Satan have any more conversations about the event that initiated the saga?

As usual, the Book of Job generates at least as many questions as answers. But the answers we do get play a significant role in helping us think and speak more accurately about God and his true nature.

As much as we call these final verses the conclusion of the story, in many ways this part of the text outlines a whole new beginning for Job. He may have thought he was living life to the fullest before the calamity, but the second phase must have felt like true life indeed. Imagine his new frame of mind for the next 140 years, seeing similar life situations from a whole new perspective. How much more did he value and appreciate the birth of each new child? How much more did he treasure every moment of life without the painful boils? How much more beautiful were the sunsets and clouds and occasional windstorms? How much more interesting did his animals seem?

Before the bomb dropped, Job was a great guy. Now he is truly enlightened, awake, and fully alive, with all his senses tuned to the majesty of God's world and to the comforting fact of being acknowledged and loved by an omnipotent Creator.

Whenever you find yourself reflecting on this great story, let your mind extend beyond the brief denouement. Let it revel in the joys now experienced by this great man who by faith survived perhaps the most extreme fiery gauntlet in human history, emerging at the other end fuller, richer, and wiser.

Imagine the testimony of God's greatness, power, and love that Job was able to share for over a century: *"I had only heard about you before, but now I have seen you with my own eyes"* (Job 42:5). His world of theological speculation was invaded by the reality of true religious experience. He found himself in a far better place.

And I'm quite sure that when Job talked to others about God for the rest of his life, he never portrayed him as merely an extremely wonderful version of himself.

REFLECTIONS

In the historical progress of divine revelation—the lengthy path God took to reveal himself and his truth to humankind—the Book of Job makes some early and notable theological contributions.

The nature of God's sovereignty is obviously a big one. Challenging our natural tendency to imagine God as just a really good human, the Book of Job boldly proclaims God as truly God—all-powerful, all-knowing, absolutely sovereign, and beyond any human control or command. He answers to no one, possesses everything, yet owes no one anything, not even an explanation for confusing circumstances.

Hence, the futility of criticizing God's ways. Not only does the text teach that God is both unpredictable and unaccountable to man, but he is running a very large and complex operation. Our present circumstantial happiness may not be his immediate and sole concern.

Some people find this reality troubling because they can only envision a God who wants everything to work out hunky-dory for them, all the time. Though they would never admit it, they pursue God on their own terms. Instead of bowing before the Lord of the universe, they think they can invite him to be their personal assistant and then scold him for not doing his job very well.

Also found in the text is a strong reminder of the remarkable power of human fortitude amidst suffering. The endurance of Job is striking. But most notable is the effect of this stamina when it's faithfully directed toward God. As I've said several times, while the friends just talked to Job *about* God, Job repeatedly talked *to* God directly. Despite his emotional outbursts and occasional rants against God for remaining silent, Job poured all his energy in God's direction. He never walked away from the Almighty or cursed him as his wife advised. To the end, Job clung to God as his only hope—in life and in death.

Because of this proper positioning, God quietly worked in his life and improved his perspective along the way, even if only in small increments. Job got better while the friends got worse. And when Job was confronted by Elihu, and then by God himself, his heart was prepared for the rebuke and he swiftly repented of the foolish things he had spoken.

The story teaches us to grant hurting souls the freedom to express their very real and raw emotions, all the while encouraging them to direct their outpouring toward God, not away from him. As well, if we seek to encourage those who suffer deeply, it is vital to bring them back repeatedly to the truth that has the power to heal: regardless of circumstance, the sovereign God of the universe is good.

Most commentators say the Book of Job deals mainly with the place of suffering within man's relationship to God. This is true, but one must never forget that Job was never privy to the heavenly conversation at the beginning of the story. Because of our backstage pass, we will always process the story differently than Job could.

Consequently, it might be more precise to say that the essence of this ancient text is more about faith and one's motives in staying true to God. Will the adversary's prediction about human behaviour come true? Are humans motivated solely to worship God as part of a give-and-get bargain? Or will Job demonstrate a faith in which one is willing to serve God for no earthly benefit?

Another central truth that springs from this tale is that man can trust God without explanation. We must accept the fact that there will always be a degree of mystery in understanding the work of God in the ebb and flow of our lives. Add to that the undisclosed activities of the spirit world, and we have a recipe for guaranteed human bewilderment.

There will be times in our lives when our circumstances make no sense. Our stories will take painful twists and turns that seem to have no rhyme or reason. On those occasions, friends will come alongside to bring comfort and encouragement. Hopefully, they'll listen carefully to our hurting hearts. With good intentions, they may try to provide answers to the complex questions that arise in times of turmoil.

But hopefully we can get to a place in our relationship with God where we can concur with G.K. Chesterton when he says, "The riddles of God are more satisfying than the solutions of man."[22]

Our questions may remain unanswered. God may appear to be silent at times, even distant. We must learn to embrace the ambiguities that confound us, realizing that our finite brains keep us from understanding eternity's fuller perspective.

Most of all, we, like Job, must learn that God's silence doesn't mean he's absent. He is always at work for our good, even though we may not be aware of it.

We also have to be impressed with Job's insights into the afterlife. Lacking the luxury of modern scripture, Job wisely concluded that the only hope for meaning in this life is the reality of an afterlife. In his highlight of faith moment, he even envisioned a future where his eternal Redeemer enabled him to live again and see God long after his earthly life had run its course.

These shreds of hope were all Job had to cling to, but they helped him get through his gut-wrenching trial. How much more should the

---

[22] "G.K. Chesterton Quotes," *Goodreads*. Date of access: March 2, 2021 (https://www.goodreads.com/quotes/189144-the-riddles-of-god-are-more-satisfying-than-the-solutions).

reality of these hopes, as fulfilled in Christ, empower believers today to survive the dark and challenging valleys of their lives?

Beyond the standard teaching points of the text, the Book of Job prompts us to ask ourselves important questions. For instance, why do we typically claim to feel God's presence when things are going well yet declare his absence when we suffer? Do we ever proclaim God to be silent when we're experiencing good times? And in those moments of loneliness and alleged abandonment, who has most likely withdrawn from the spiritual engagement—God or us?

On another note, what *do* we truly deserve in this life? Do we deserve that things go well for us because we've put in a decent effort to walk obediently with the Lord? Do we truly expect God to intercept every hurricane, tornado, tidal wave, stock market collapse, drunk driver, speeding bullet, or falling rock that careens in our direction? Can he only be considered loving and just if he does so? What role does the free will of man play in our suffering? How does the fact that our world is damaged by sin play into our narratives of hardship and disappointment? Furthermore, what does it take to feel the love of God when we are in pain?

Or are we asking the wrong questions altogether? Instead of "Why me?" maybe it should be "Why not me?" And instead of asking endless angst-filled *why* questions, maybe we should put more effort into believing that God's grace is sufficient for our troubles, that his power is made perfect in our weakness (2 Corinthians 12:9), and that, as the psalmist says, his way is perfect (Psalm 18:30).

This calm and complete space, this place of rest, is where I believe Job was able to land. Before the tragedies, Job would have considered his life to be very decent. But as Harold Kushner puts it, "There is something unripe about the person who has never tasted disappointment or sorrow."[23] Job was an incredible guy at the begin-

---

[23] Kushner, *The Book of Job*, 131.

ning of the story. But he still had room to grow. There were more precious metals of character to purify. There existed the potential for a closer connection with God that comes only through brokenness and divine healing.

Before, like his friends, Job knew his theology. Afterward, he truly knew his God. Before, incongruities in life demanded an explanation. Afterward, all questions became moot. Once you truly meet God and experience a close personal connection with him, the circumstantial matters of life shrink in comparison.

Sin is the most significant aspect of our lives that hinders our close connection with God. You see, the Book of Job doesn't just present a philosophical problem that needs resolving; it showcases a heart problem that needs repentance: human sin must be exposed and dealt with.

Job recognized the propensity of the next generation to fade spiritually through the deceptiveness of sin. Hence, he wisely offered sacrifices for his children after they partied together, in case any of them had sinned against God or cursed him in their hearts.

What did he think about the potential for sin in his own life before his world imploded? The text doesn't reveal much about that. God called him blameless, but no human in this life is perfect. Still, I think it's safe to assume that since Job cared a great deal about his children's integrity, he was committed to keeping short accounts with God regarding his own behaviour.

But as the waves of terror began to crash upon him, Job continued to say the right things until he couldn't. No matter how pure we are, there will always be a root of bitterness hidden within the human heart. The blameless, upstanding Job began to sin with his mouth by declaring God unjust and by demanding explanations. Though they were more subtle than the overt crimes we abhor, Job's sins had to be dealt with as well.

As for the friends? Well, they sinned all over the place. Not only did they speak inaccurately about God, they also trashed their friend at his lowest point. Their greatest sin was probably their failure to be the true comforters God intended them to be in this tragic situation. Ignorantly, they said that God was punishing Job for his sin. While God was doing a good work in Job's life, the friends self-righteously revelled in their own counterfeit security, belittling the complexity of God's goodness and sovereignty. Friends who suffer need merciful comforters, not arrogant know-it-all theologians. And as we saw, the sins of these silly stubborn scholars had to be addressed and confessed.

Repentance of sin is an important theme in the Book of Job, and it continues to be so throughout all of Scripture. The Apostle Paul, referring to himself as the chief of sinners, was obviously concerned about the topic of repentance. As was Jesus.

Luke the evangelist wrote the following in his New Testament Gospel:

> *About this time Jesus was informed that Pilate had murdered some people from Galilee as they were offering sacrifices at the Temple. "Do you think those Galileans were worse sinners than all the other people from Galilee?" Jesus asked. "Is that why they suffered? Not at all! And you will perish, too, unless you repent of your sins and turn to God. And what about the eighteen people who died when the tower in Siloam fell on them? Were they the worst sinners in Jerusalem? No, and I tell you again that unless you repent, you will perish, too."*
>
> —Luke 13:1–5

This passage sounds like Jesus making a commentary on the Book of Job. Bad circumstances don't automatically imply the guilt of the victims. We will rarely discern the exact purpose of disasters in this world, but the right answer for humans in every circumstance is possessing an attitude of humility and repentance.

Completely out of vogue with the values of this world, a humble heart and willingness to repent are far more important issues than length of life or our level of comfort. In the eyes of God, the real problem we should be concerned about is our sin, not the supposed problem of the existence of evil and suffering in a world governed by a good God.

Suffering is part of the messiness of a fallen, unredeemed world. The Apostle Paul says that *"the whole creation groans"* (Romans 8:22, NASB). And as people bellow "Where was God when Hurricane Katrina struck?" or "Where is God in the spread of COVID-19" our response should be, "Right where he always is: whispering in the ears of the volunteers rescuing those stranded on rooftops, inspiring those who respond to the call of comforting those who mourn, and strengthening the resilience of the tired, overworked medical professionals who care for the sick." It has been said that the task of true religion is to sweeten the bitter water, not question why God allowed it to be bitter in the first place. I like that.

It is understandable, though. I get it. At times we may wonder how God can truly love us and still allow so much pain in our lives. But it really does depend on how we view *love*, doesn't it? God's love isn't just an easy breezy feeling of infatuation. It's something far deeper and richer, something that cherishes and disciplines, hurts and heals. In fact, God's love is always best displayed amidst pain and hardship.

Just hours before his crucifixion, Jesus told his followers, *"There is no greater love than to lay down one's life for one's friends"* (John 15:13). God loves us so much that he gave up his own Son to die on the cross to show it. Jesus loves us so much that he was willing to stay on the cross until his Father's plan was complete.

And look what his love has won for those who choose to believe and follow: freedom from a life of selfishness and sin, a reconciled relationship with our Creator, and the blessed hope of eternal joy in his presence.

When we ponder the depth of God's love and realize what that love has secured for us, how dare we question his motives as he sovereignly directs our paths? If he loved us enough to die for us, surely he can be trusted in the middle of our pain and problems—and trusted not just to deliver us *from* our sorrows, but to deliver us and perfect us *through* our sorrows.

FINAL THOUGHTS

The big picture plans and purposes of God are clearly revealed in Scripture. Being born ignorant and naturally rebellious, we are drawn by God through various forms of revelation to acknowledge and embrace him as Creator, Saviour, and Lord. As the ultimate Ruler of Everything, he invites us to join his eternal Kingdom through faith in his Son Jesus whose death and resurrection defeated sin and death. Ultimately, God desires that we enjoy an eternal state with him forever—the meeting of heaven and earth, Creator and creation in perfect unity.

But between points A and B, there is life to be lived, a path to be trod. On that path, we discover many pleasures as well as frequent sorrows. As we travel this trail of delights and disappointments, progressing toward our final union with God, we ponder both his nature and the nature of our journey. Depending on the ease of the pilgrimage, we make summary assessments about who God is and how he relates to us in our present position.

In our study of Job, we have endeavoured to gain a more accurate understanding of God's sovereignty and love. In the process, God's transcendence and benevolence have been brought to the fore.

Ultimately, it becomes clear to Job that even though there are no limitations on what the Lord can do, there is also no threshold on his love for humankind. Even beyond the confines of the Book of

Job itself, it is unmistakable that both God's sovereignty and love are repeatedly displayed in every corner of his good creation.

As we attempt to grasp the vastness of the universe and mind-boggling structure of the atom, we cannot help but conclude that our Creator is frighteningly powerful. And as we see how God weaves the intricate tapestry of human history and directs the tiny particles within the operation of a living cell so our hearts keep beating, we cannot help but marvel at his compassionate care.

But when the path of our own lives goes awry, we often struggle to harmonize the dual concepts of God's power and goodness.

In the face of this intellectual challenge, two faulty lines of thinking commonly emerge. Some earnest believers put themselves under the unrealistic pressure of trying to get it all figured out, largely to no avail. Others adopt the error of trying to make the paradox more human-friendly and palatable.

In contrast to these poor approaches, I have advocated for a humble acceptance of the enigmatic. If we're honest, we must concede that the balance of God's goodness and sovereign power will always carry a measure of mystery. The logistics of God's work in this world remain beyond human comprehension because they are divine.

The modern mindset is very reluctant to tolerate divine mystery. Fooled into thinking we can understand everything, we struggle to concede that we will never fully grasp God's transcendence this side of heaven. Consequently, we tend to mentally fashion a Divine Being out of our own imagination that works for us personally. Within our comfortable homemade images of God, the presence of pain and evil make us uncomfortable.

In pre-modern times in the West, people acknowledged suffering in the world, but they never made it an argument against the existence of a good God. Now we are drunk with what James K.A. Smith refers to as a modern-day "confidence in our powers of exhaustive surveillance."[24] In other words, because we can't think of any good reason why God would allow suffering in the world, we conclude that there can't be one.

Logically, this argument is silly. Theologically, how dare we reduce the Infinite One to our mere finite understanding of him? God's ways are far beyond our paygrade. He does complex things in the realm of human experience that are off our radar. So many things are out of our control, completely beyond us.

Like Job, we need to get it by acknowledging that we don't get it. Just like we cannot grasp the magnitude of his sovereign creative power within our gigantic universe, we also cannot fathom his sovereign works of sustenance, empowerment, healing, encouragement, comfort, renewal, and forgiveness in our lives.

Even though it is at times inexplicable and inscrutable, God's benevolent power is real, and undeniable. Countless are the testimonies of the Lord's faithful servants who have been delivered both *from* and *through* their trials by our loving Creator. For centuries, the witness of the saints has been consistent—God is powerful, and he is good, in times of ease and comfort, and in days of darkness.

It is ironic. Repeatedly, we use divine terms to describe God in our general theological discussions, but then we use human terms to evaluate him in our own circumstances. We're comfortable throwing around celestial superlatives when the topic at hand doesn't touch us personally. But when the pain hits home, when we assess the degree of our own personal suffering or vent our disappointment with life in general, we often treat God like he is a human who has let us down.

The line of thinking is common: "Unlike our nice neighbour down the street who always does what he can to help us out, God didn't come through for us in our particular situation, in our time of desperate need. He didn't show up, and tragedy struck. We prayed,

---

[24] James K.A. Smith, *How (Not) to Be Secular: Reading Charles Taylor* (Grand Rapids, MI: Eerdmans, 2014), 65.

but I guess he wasn't listening. He didn't prevent what he could have prevented, so how can I believe he is all-powerful? I don't get it; if God truly is a God of love, shouldn't he be nicer? If I had more power, I would certainly use it to alleviate as much pain and suffering as possible. Surely God should behave at least as nice as I would."

There is much that could be said in response to this popular human paradigm, but suffice it to say that such an assessment is flawed because it portrays God merely as a really good human.

Oh, we would never admit to such blasphemy. But we are guilty. We do it all the time. This is where our minds go when we struggle with our faith. We turn the nature of God into a checklist of all the best human ideas we've come up with so far.

We limit our concept of God's love to our finest earthly images of gushy sentiment. We reduce our perception of God's goodness to our best human descriptions of being nice. We confine our understanding of God's sovereignty to similes of human control, like a construction worker operating a crane with levers. We narrow down God's holiness to our strongest human images of good behaviour. We dilute God's wrath to a flavour resembling human bitterness, resentment, and anger. And then we shape his omnipotence into the human notion of doing everything possible within our limitations—for example, if God were to decide finally to start doing it right, he would use his infinite power to fix every problem that exists in the world, immediately.

In sum, we want God to behave the way we think an excellent human would behave. This is a mistake. Don't confuse the truth of us being created in God's image with the faulty notion of him being the best version of ourselves. God is not the top-of-the-line model of humanity. Though he imminently works within us, he is transcendent and unequalled in his character.

Back in the day, God's transcendence was a more natural fit for the average human heart. Life was a bit simpler and the stars at night confirmed what the brain had been taught by parents and the church: *There is a God, and he is very big and beyond anything our mind can fully capture.* But in our postmodern world, with all its sophistication, hedonism, and expressive individualism, it takes a tall order of faith and humility to conceptualize God properly.

We need to swim strongly against the current of contemporary western culture to even believe in God, let alone believe in the God Job came to know—a good, loving, omnipotent God who might test us at levels beyond what we think we can handle. Surviving those tests, fortunately, doesn't take a PhD in astrophysics, but it does require faith—faith to believe that God is compassionate, merciful, and always working for our good regardless of the quality of our living conditions.

One New Testament writer puts it this way: *"And it is impossible to please God without faith. Anyone who wants to come to him must believe that God exists and that he rewards those who sincerely seek him"* (Hebrews 11:6).

Many spiritual pilgrims embark on the journey of seeking God for these promised rewards, but the outcome of the effort depends on the type of God they pursue. Searching for a deity of our own making is effortless. We can erroneously conclude that he's right there inside our own imagination, easy to understand and committed to doing our bidding. But be warned: such a deity will have no life-changing power because he doesn't really exist, except in our own minds.

On the contrary, the work involved in sincerely seeking the one true God of the universe requires some heavy-lifting. We may have to give up certain notions about God that have kept us comfortable for many years. We may have to accept certain truths about the Almighty that threaten to make us uncomfortable going forward.

But even though God graciously allows us to know him intimately, we must acknowledge that there are no prescribed formulas for an easy ride during the journey, no guaranteed stress-free luxury berths on the train. Many, like Job, reach their deepest intimacy with God through the breaking power of tragedies and whirlwinds, life-changing and even fearful events that provide glimpses of the Lord's awesome majesty and glory.

As our young friends in *The Lion, the Witch, and the Wardrobe* came to understand from Mrs. Beaver, "If there's anyone who can appear before [God] without their knees knocking, they're either braver than most or else just silly."[25] C.S. Lewis had it right, and Job would certainly agree: those who resolve to pursue the Lord of the universe with their whole heart need to be ready to embrace an all-powerful God who is good, but not necessarily safe.

---

[25] Lewis, *The Lion, the Witch and the Wardrobe*, 75.

ABOUT THE AUTHOR

Dwight Olney grew up in Kitchener, Ontario as the son of a piano tuner. At fifteen, he moved to Alberta when his father became the pastor of a church in the small northern community of Lac La Biche.

After high school, Dwight trained to become a secondary school teacher, focusing on history and mathematics. After fifteen years in the classroom, he worked sixteen more as an in-school administrator for the Prairie South School Division in southern Saskatchewan.

The bulk of his formal education has focused on the study of theology (Briercrest College), history (University of Waterloo), education (Queen's University), and administration (Jones International University).

Dwight finds great joy in teaching, preaching, carpentry, recreational hockey, and coaching basketball. He has three married children and has been blessed with three beautiful grandchildren.

His theological skills have been honed through studying and teaching the Bible as an adult Sunday school teacher, preacher, author, and principal of a private Christian high school.

His fondest area of interest is practical theology, where he loves to challenge people to think in new ways by recognizing faulty human thought lines and replacing them with God-like thinking.

Dwight now lives with his patient and understanding wife, Jeanette, in Winnipeg, Manitoba.

Information regarding Dwight's other books can be found at www.mindrenovation.com. For all other communication, feel free to contact him at dwightolney@gmail.com.

Also by the Author

Master Mind challenges readers to undergo a mind renovation, where weak, faulty, and deceptive human thought patterns are torn out and replaced with God-like thinking. The work is principally based on Paul's instructions in Romans 12:2 to *"let God transform you into a new person by changing the way you think"* (NLT). *Master Mind* provides a fresh perspective on a broad spectrum of topics ranging from apologetics and divine paradox to body modification and human sexuality. It is a useful resource of practical theology designed both for personal learning and for study within a discipleship class or adult small group.

Mind Renovation continues the challenge offered in *Master* Mind—to encourage and equip readers to step out of their natural human thought patterns and find a better life and stronger relationship with God by aligning their thinking with the mind of the Creator. Like that old house that inspires one renovation project after another, the process of our own mind renovation is an ongoing venture. Similar to *Master Mind, Mind Renovation* covers a wide range of topics from servanthood and intolerance to fatherhood and dying well.

Because the default setting of the natural mind is geared towards independence from God, those desiring to know our Heavenly Father must be mindful of the temptation to pursue him according to their own plans. Sincere spiritual seekers want to know God intimately. But in their effort to draw close to the Almighty, many of these seekers often disobey God in the process. Such a practice can be referred to as *Sacred Sedition*. It is sacred because it involves the pursuit of God. It is seditious because that pursuit is executed contrary to God's instructions.

www.ingramcontent.com/pod-product-compliance
Lightning Source LLC
Chambersburg PA
CBHW062106080426
42734CB00012B/2776